The GOOD OLD DAYS

A Reflection upon What we Individually and Collectively Choose NOT to Recall

BY
RICK SPLEEN

THE GOOD OLD DAYS: A REFLECTION UPON WHAT WE INDIVIDUALLY AND COLLECTIVELY CHOOSE NOT TO RECALL

1405 SW 6th Avenue • Ocala, Florida 34471 • Phone 352-622-1825 • Fax 352-622-1875
Website: www.atlantic-pub.com • Email: sales@atlantic-pub.com
SAN Number: 268-1250

Library of Congress Control Number: 2020912382

Printed in the United States

PROJECT MANAGER: Kassandra White
INTERIOR LAYOUT AND JACKET DESIGN: Nicole Sturk

*To all those who came before me and made possible this moment in time.
Their efforts and innovation afforded me the leisure for this and other pursuits,
as well as the countless modern conveniences I take advantage of each day.*

*To my father and mother, Jack and Sue, without whom I would not exist.
Their nurture in my formative years and their tolerance and guidance in later
years have made all things possible.*

*It is with considerable regret that Jack is no longer with us to read
what I have put here to paper.*

*Finally, to my daughter, Bella, who gives life and the word Love meaning for me.
My little Princess; she is "the only one."*

*Hopefully one day she will read my work,
as well as some of the many other books I have given her through the years.*

The
GOOD OLD DAYS

A Reflection upon what we
Individually and Collectively
Choose NOT to Recall

Contents

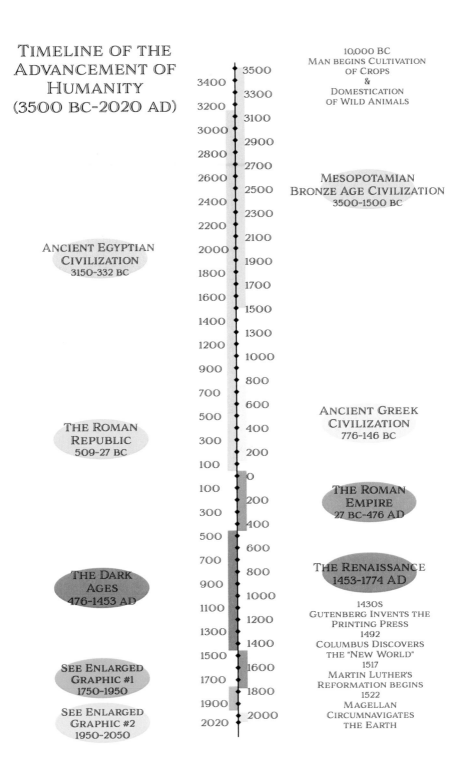

Timeline of the Advancement of Humanity (3500 BC-2020 AD)

10,000 BC
Man begins Cultivation
of Crops
&
Domestication
of Wild Animals

Mesopotamian
Bronze Age Civilization
3500-1500 BC

Ancient Egyptian
Civilization
3150-332 BC

The Roman
Republic
509-27 BC

Ancient Greek
Civilization
776-146 BC

The Roman
Empire
27 BC-476 AD

The Dark
Ages
476-1453 AD

The Renaissance
1453-1774 AD

1430s
Gutenberg Invents the
Printing Press
1492
Columbus Discovers
the "New World"
1517
Martin Luther's
Reformation Begins
1522
Magellan
Circumnavigates
the Earth

See Enlarged
Graphic #1
1750-1950

See Enlarged
Graphic #2
1950-2050

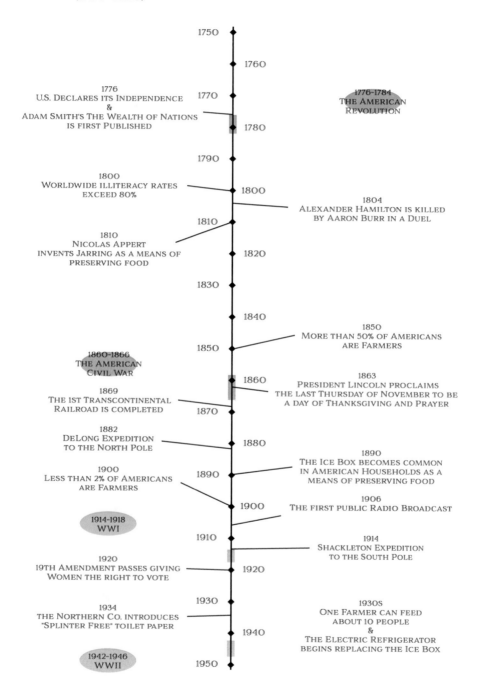

ENLARGED GRAPHIC #1
(1750-1950)

1750

1760

1776
U.S. DECLARES ITS INDEPENDENCE   1770
&
ADAM SMITH'S THE WEALTH OF NATIONS
IS FIRST PUBLISHED   1780

1776-1784
THE AMERICAN
REVOLUTION

1790

1800
WORLDWIDE ILLITERACY RATES   1800
EXCEED 80%

1804
ALEXANDER HAMILTON IS KILLED
BY AARON BURR IN A DUEL

1810

1810
NICOLAS APPERT
INVENTS JARRING AS A MEANS OF   1820
PRESERVING FOOD

1830

1840

1850
MORE THAN 50% OF AMERICANS
ARE FARMERS

1850

1860-1866
THE AMERICAN
CIVIL WAR

1860

1863
PRESIDENT LINCOLN PROCLAIMS
THE LAST THURSDAY OF NOVEMBER TO BE
A DAY OF THANKSGIVING AND PRAYER

1869
THE 1ST TRANSCONTINENTAL
RAILROAD IS COMPLETED   1870

1882
DELONG EXPEDITION
TO THE NORTH POLE   1880

1890
THE ICE BOX BECOMES COMMON
IN AMERICAN HOUSEHOLDS AS A
MEANS OF PRESERVING FOOD

1900
LESS THAN 2% OF AMERICANS   1890
ARE FARMERS

1906
THE FIRST PUBLIC RADIO BROADCAST

1900

1914-1918
WWI

1910

1914
SHACKLETON EXPEDITION
TO THE SOUTH POLE

1920
19TH AMENDMENT PASSES GIVING   1920
WOMEN THE RIGHT TO VOTE

1930

1934
THE NORTHERN CO. INTRODUCES
"SPLINTER FREE" TOILET PAPER

1930S
ONE FARMER CAN FEED
ABOUT 10 PEOPLE
&
THE ELECTRIC REFRIGERATOR
BEGINS REPLACING THE ICE BOX

1940

1942-1946
WWII   1950

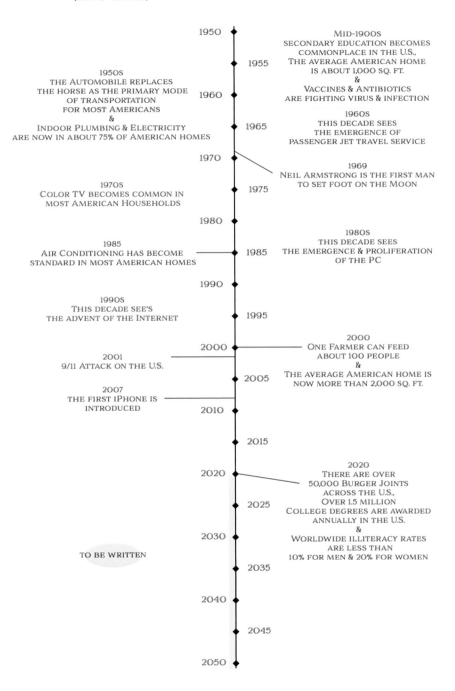

ENLARGED GRAPHIC #2
(1950-2050)

1950

MID-1900S
SECONDARY EDUCATION BECOMES
COMMONPLACE IN THE U.S.,
THE AVERAGE AMERICAN HOME
IS ABOUT 1,000 SQ. FT.
&
VACCINES & ANTIBIOTICS
ARE FIGHTING VIRUS & INFECTION

1955

1960

1950S
THE AUTOMOBILE REPLACES
THE HORSE AS THE PRIMARY MODE
OF TRANSPORTATION
FOR MOST AMERICANS
&
INDOOR PLUMBING & ELECTRICITY
ARE NOW IN ABOUT 75% OF AMERICAN HOMES

1965

1960S
THIS DECADE SEES
THE EMERGENCE OF
PASSENGER JET TRAVEL SERVICE

1970

1975

1969
NEIL ARMSTRONG IS THE FIRST MAN
TO SET FOOT ON THE MOON

1970S
COLOR TV BECOMES COMMON IN
MOST AMERICAN HOUSEHOLDS

1980

1985
AIR CONDITIONING HAS BECOME
STANDARD IN MOST AMERICAN HOMES

1985

1980S
THIS DECADE SEES
THE EMERGENCE & PROLIFERATION
OF THE PC

1990

1990S
THIS DECADE SEE'S
THE ADVENT OF THE INTERNET

1995

2000

2000
ONE FARMER CAN FEED
ABOUT 100 PEOPLE
&
THE AVERAGE AMERICAN HOME IS
NOW MORE THAN 2,000 SQ. FT.

2001
9/11 ATTACK ON THE U.S.

2005

2007
THE FIRST iPHONE IS
INTRODUCED

2010

2015

2020

2020
THERE ARE OVER
50,000 BURGER JOINTS
ACROSS THE U.S.,
OVER 1.5 MILLION
COLLEGE DEGREES ARE AWARDED
ANNUALLY IN THE U.S.
&
WORLDWIDE ILLITERACY RATES
ARE LESS THAN
10% FOR MEN & 20% FOR WOMEN

2025

2030

2035

TO BE WRITTEN

2040

2045

2050

Prologue

⮰

For many years now, I've contemplated statements that have been used with increasing regularity in the public domain, but to my understanding bear no basis in fact. In the 1990s one in particular had come into prominence, and since then has moved to the forefront in the heightened political debate over the healthcare legislation that was passed by the House of Representatives on March 21, 2010. This statement, which has been used by many in the media as well as many prominent public officials, has principally taken the following two forms:

- ❖ Access to quality healthcare is a basic human right, or
- ❖ Access to affordable healthcare is a basic human right.

Both the words "quality" and "affordable" are entirely subjective, and any attempt to quantify them in the contexts used above is relative to any one individual's perspective. Who should we look to as the arbitrator of what represents "quality" and/or "affordable"? Moreover, when these phrases are used, the discourse that follows has little to do with quality and/or affordability. The focus is immediately redirected toward insurance coverage, which has little, if any, correlation to either. Of the many questions that such proclamations should give rise to, foremost should be the question of who we believe affords us our basic human rights: The Government? What was Jefferson thinking when he wrote that we "are endowed by [our] Creator with certain unalienable Rights, that among these are Life, Liberty, and the Pursuit of Happiness"? Could Moses have misplaced the Creator's proclamation on "Quality/Affordable Healthcare" when he came down from Mount Sinai to deliver the Ten Commandments?

One can only ponder that, as a basic human right, this issue surely must have weighed heavily on George Washington's mind as he set off to lead the Continental Army in 1775, through those long winter nights at Morristown and Valley Forge, and throughout the duration of his six-year campaign against the British Crown. Surely it was a major consideration for James Madison as he set out for the Constitutional Convention in 1887 with the Virginia Plan to forge a new government, although he must have misplaced the provision on Healthcare when the Bill of Rights was later adopted. And surely it was a hot topic during the many spirited debates between Jefferson and Hamilton in the first administration. As humorous as you may find the foregoing, it should be equally as comical for anyone to put forth such rhetoric today, and yet it persists, often without challenge.

I sometimes wonder of George Washington's reaction if we could somehow travel back in time and meet him during his first administration. While a discussion of subsequent industrial and technical advancements, the expansion of the Union to the Pacific and 50 states, or the abolition of slavery are most likely not unique topics to be contemplated as part of the discourse, what may be unique are topics that could be viewed as the major political issues being contemplated and debated publically and in our government today. Try to picture our first president, after having commanded the continental army, "a rabble in rags," in a six-year struggle against the British Empire, the greatest military force at that time, and now mediating the debates between Hamilton and Jefferson over how to handle the debt from that war. Now imagine that you are in that room, and you advise the Commander-in-Chief that some 200 years in the future the national debt exceeds $20 trillion dollars and continues to grow at a rate of approximately a trillion dollars a year. The fact that this issue of the debt is taking a backseat to other issues taking prominence should be of greater concern in both public and political circles. Instead there are issues such as the question of whether a man should be able to marry another man or the need for transgender bathrooms. Upon hearing those words, the quarreling over vastly differing of opinions between Hamilton and Jefferson would most likely have melted away and vanished, and George, after having restrained an initial desire to give you a taste of cold steel and run you through, would most likely write you off for your foolishness.

Another of the mantras that has permeated our lexicon for some time now is the stated view that the current or next generation will be the first generation that will not be better off than its predecessor. While this view will be readily dispelled in the chapters that follow, I find it difficult to restrain my desire to address it here. How could anyone consider their prospects in life to compare with that of the generation coming off the Roaring Twenties to experience the Great Depression, only to continue their life through World War II?

You may be familiar with the characterization of someone living in a bubble. Apart from the literal application, it is typically applied to public officials in high office or senior executives in private sector business, wherein the information that a politician or an executive bases his decisions and/or actions upon is limited to that filtered to him by those whom he surrounds himself with. The same can be applied to any one of us. In a micro sense, each of our own bubbles consist of all the sources of information that we limit ourselves to, and in a macro sense, they consist of the cumulative sum of all the information that we absorb in our lifetimes. We all live in our own little bubbles of time and space, some reinforcing the environment of their bubbles while others expand that environment to varying degrees.

Throughout the history of mankind, measuring back over a million years, man has lived a meager hand-to-mouth existence, at least for a vast majority of this time. Only within the past few thousand years with the advent of civilization did some begin to emerge from this common fate, and then only a relative few. From the earliest days in Mesopotamia, through the Egyptian, Greek, and Roman civilizations, regressing in the Dark Ages and reemerging with the Renaissance, only a select and very small few emerged from this dismal existence as the nobility of their times. It was not until the emergence of the Industrial Age in the late 1800s that spawned the beginnings of what we today refer to as a middle class. Before that, there were the *Haves* (a small fraction of a percent of the population), and the *Have Nots* (the masses, or everyone else). But before venturing further, we need to place into context these two types of existence for these periods of civilization.

❖ The *Haves* - Nobility, ruling, and/or the landholding class. Kings, lords, emperors, senators, pharaohs etc. and their respective immediate underlings, sometimes including the upper echelon of the respective religious hierarchy. Their standard of living could hardly be considered equal to even those who we may refer to as the more modest of today's middle class. This was their fate generation after generation, through the centuries, with little opportunity to change their station in life, except through violent struggle, which may lead to marginal improvement, but more often than not it led to a far worse fate.

❖ The ***Have Nots*** - For the most part, this included everyone else, which included slaves (it has been estimated that nearly a third of the population of ancient Rome were slaves). If not literally slaves (the outright property of others), whether called peasants, serfs, or simply farmers, these people toiled and worked land that they did not own for a meager hand-to-mouth existence until the day they died in obscurity. This was their fate generation after generation, through the centuries, with absolutely no opportunity to change their station in life.

For the millennia of mankind's existence, before the founding of the United States and well into the early years of the American Experiment, daily life for the masses was as miserable as that of a stray cat, scavenging through garbage to subside on a bitter cold and rainy night. It was not until the Enlightenment leading into the Industrial Revolution in the late 1700s through the early 1800s that this continuum began to change. Coincidentally, at the same time a fledgling democracy in the form of a republic was born in the New World. One which proclaimed that "all Men are created equal, that they are endowed by their Creator with certain unalienable Rights, that among these are Life, Liberty, and the Pursuit of Happiness." It was with this freedom that the engine of capitalism accelerated the evolution of prosperity that we know today.

In the chapters that follow, I shall endeavor to put forth evidence in support of my firm belief that irrespective of one's station in life, life is indeed good and, moreover, uniformly exceeds that of any period that has come before us by nearly any measure, and in many cases by considerable measure. The lion's share of the advancements leading to this prosperity, by and large, have come about in little less than the last 250 years, and this rapid acceleration in prosperity is inseparably linked to the founding of the United States of America, the freedoms the republic affords us by its creation, and, as an extension of those rights, the Nation's Free Enterprise or Capitalistic economy that made it all possible. Unleashed by this liberty is what had come to be known as the "Protestant work ethic," giving rise to and driving initiative and innovation, all of which are inherent in the human spirit to varying degrees and are readily invigorated by Free Enterprise and stifled by Socialism.

Chapter 1

The Necessities of Life

"Necessity is the mother of invention."

—*Author unknown, but its genius is
generally attributed to Plato*

When I was a senior in high school, not just one of my favorites but my favorite teacher was a man by the name of Chester Rohrbach (Chet), who taught a class called "Problems of Democracy" or as we referred to it POD. One of the many interesting things about Chet was that although he was not one of the younger, cool teachers, his presence alone seemed enough to capture the attention of his students as soon as he entered the room. He was an older gentleman and a gentleman in every sense of the word. Honor and integrity were not just words to Chet, and he approached teaching as a personal responsibility to transition us from a bunch of juvenile high school seniors to knowledgeable and responsible citizens. Besides teaching the standard curriculum, the base of which was the formation, makeup, and functioning of our national, state, and local governments, he brought to bear his own life experiences in anecdotal form. While the degree to which these stories supported what he was teaching in class on a given day varied, they succeeded in capturing and retaining my and my classmates' attention. He had what seemed to be a lot to draw upon, years where the standard modes of transportation were the railroad and trolley, the Great Depression, service in World War II, the pride he took in his alma mater,

Penn State (where I would later go on to receive my college education also), and, one of his favorites, his youth and growing up on a farm. He instilled in us the appreciation he gained from a simple life on that farm, and for what the Almighty provided. Lost today is the reality of having to kill and butcher the chicken or other livestock that would provide the meal on your table.

One story that has stayed with me was when he told us that on the farm where he grew up, there was no bathroom as we know it. There was an outhouse, and while we all knew what an outhouse was, until that time I do not believe any of the students in my class (1976) appreciated the ramifications of what it was like for an outhouse to be part of your everyday life. Try to imagine, with all your senses, the aroma, which on hot summer days was all the more accentuated.

THE OUTHOUSE – A quintessential part of early American life, they were a prominent feature across the American landscape well into the 1900s. In fact, the WPA built more than two million outhouses in the United States during the Great Depression years.

Also, in summer, there was the companionship of flies, insects, and other creepy crawly things, sometimes in considerable numbers. Or, in the depth of winter, when Mother Nature calls, the need to go forced you to venture out into the elements no matter how extreme. Irrespective of the season, now try to comprehend the complement of these experiences at night, or early morning, in the dark.

Somewhere in all of this, he made mention of a pile of corncobs in the outhouse, the use of which required an explanation by Chet for many in my class (for those readers that also require an explanation: before or in the absence of toilet paper, corncobs that were left over from feeding the pigs, were saved and stacked in the outhouse for later use in cleaning up after your business was complete). Unfortunately, I do not recall the context into which all of this fell in our lesson for that day, but what I do recall – and what made this an indelible imprint on my memory – was the reaction of that group of adolescents, who were my classmates. If you've been around groups of teenagers, and who hasn't, you've undoubtedly seen it: a combination of shock, awe, and amazement coupled with giggles and laughter sometimes, and in this case to an extreme. For many, if not all in my class, including myself, this revelation was met with comic relief on the surface, and the deeper reality was that such a thing was beyond the realm of our comprehension. Certainly this was not a part of our world, and it's almost impossible to relate to for any subsequent generation. It was however, a very real part of daily life in Chet's youth, one of which he spoke of in a simple, matter-of-fact manner.

As I recall, it got me thinking at the time that this was a part of life for a man only one generation removed from my own, and yet it seemed worlds apart. When did something as simple as toilet paper come into existence? Something that until that time I took totally for granted as part of my daily life. This thought crossed my mind some 40 years ago, which of course was well before the advent of the internet, without which, how could anyone research such a subject? Furthermore, at that point in my life, I was surely consumed by many better and more pressing things to do with my time (intended satirically). As it turns out, I now have the time, the motivation (not exactly sure why), and the internet at my fingertips, not only to contemplate such things, but also to find some of the answers. In an effort to satisfy curious minds such as my own, here's what I found:

Although the existence of forms of toilet paper are recorded much earlier in history, it did not come into commercial existence until the late 1800s, and it does not appear to have gained widespread commercial and public acceptance as a consumer product until the early 1900s. There appear to be two major reasons for the almost fifty-year delay in its acceptance and widespread use. The first being the fact that this topic, and in turn such products, were a very taboo subject for people of the Victorian Era. While this may seem odd to us today, it is easily understood when you consider that a product seemingly so essential in our everyday lives is rarely a topic of any conversation. You need only to give little thought to the alternatives, and you will realize it receives nowhere near the credit it deserves. Today, with the Victorian Era well behind us, toilet paper is now advertised openly and regularly on many platforms, including television, although neither Mr. Wipple or others peddling the product make any mention of how or what it is used for. The second issue delaying its acceptance was simply the refinement of the product itself. One issue, and of very real concern, was the potential of splinters (Ouch!) as a result of the crude manufacturing of the period. It was not until the 1930s that Northern Co. introduced and advertised its toilet paper as "Splinter Free." Until this time, and through the period that toilet paper was gaining general acceptance, things such as rags, newspapers, leaves, corncobs, etc. were most commonly used. In the absence of any of these, people would use their hand and water. Hopefully some soap was also available at the appropriate time.

This ad by the Northern Tissue Co. promotes their innovation of "Splinter Free" Toilet Paper. It appeared in the March 1935 edition of the *Ladies Home Journal. Used with permission of Georgia Pacific LLC. All rights reserved.*

This ad by the Northern Tissue Co. also promoting their "Splinter Free" Toilet Paper appeared in the July 1934 edition of the *Ladies Home Journal*. It illustrates the subtleties of advertising the advantages of their product in a period still dominated by Victorian morals. *Used with permission of Georgia Pacific LLC. All rights reserved.*

There was another item that caught favor in America prior to the acceptance and widespread use of commercial toilet paper. Almost in parallel with the development of commercial toilet paper, the Sears and Roebuck Co. began widespread "free" distribution of its famous catalog to rural America in the late 1890s. It wasn't long before this catalog found its way into the outhouses of America, as reading material during the daily constitutional of these Americans. Well before toilet paper found its way into these outhouses, as new editions of the Sears Catalog were published, the outdated copies of the catalog doubled in their usefulness as a substitute for the corncobs. At over 700 pages, an old copy of the Sears catalog could provide an individual a year's worth of wipes. With the larger families of the day, it surely had a much shorter life in the outhouses across the American countryside.

Beyond toilet paper, there are many other modern conveniences that we readily take for granted, and I truly believe that many who live in their bubble of modern life just assume they were a part of civilized society for considerable time. They are numerous, ubiquitous, and in most cases have come to the common man in very recent generations. I'm not referring to the advent of television, or the smart phone, or other more notable, obvious, and recent innovations that many may view as a necessary part of their modern lives and casually say they could not live without but are in fact little more than distractions from reality. Like toilet paper, I'm referring to the many things we use daily with little thought of how essential they are in making the realities of humanity tolerable in our modern society. Some of the more prominent in my view include, but are by no means limited to:

- ❖ The Flush Toilet
- ❖ General Sanitation and Personal Hygiene
- ❖ Fresh Hot and Cold Running Water

❖ Heating and Cooling

❖ Lighting

❖ Transportation

❖ Clothing and Fashion

❖ Feminine Hygiene and the Disposable Diaper

The Flush Toilet is another innovation that for similar reasons is taken for granted quite literally as much as toilet paper. This fixture, whose development is tied to the advent of indoor plumbing, was originally conceived in the late 1500s but didn't find its way into popular use until the 1850s. Although common urban legend tributes the invention of the flush toilet to Thomas Crapper, the credit actually goes to an Englishman by the name of John Harrington. It was Thomas Crapper, another English plumber, who some 300 years later brought the fixture into popular use with other plumbing fixtures, such as wash basins and bath tubs, in conjunction with modern indoor plumbing. Not to minimize the importance of these other fixtures, but in the end, it was the flush toilet that his name became somewhat synonymous with. The initial popularity of the flush toilet remained somewhat isolated to England until around the time of the first World War (1914 to 1918). Among the first Americans to experience the use of a flush toilet were some of the millions of GIs who arrived in England during that war.

Prior to flush toilets coming into the home, there were few alternatives. As cited in the above narrative on toilet paper, the outhouse was prominent throughout early rural America. However, outhouses were rarely practical in more densely populated urban centers. In the cities, before the toilet and indoor plumbing, the answer to your needs was provided by the most simplistic of devices. It was called a "chamber pot." For the common folk, it could take the form of little more than a metal bucket, and for those with means it could be ornately decorated porcelain or china. Chamber pots were generally kept out of view in the bedroom, under the bed, but needed to be emptied and cleaned, for obvious reasons, daily after use. Without indoor

THE CHAMBER POT – Neatly and inconspicuously tucked away under the foot of the bed, this accessory was commonly used in more urban settings or in rural settings as an alternative to trekking out into the elements during inclement weather.

plumbing this was typically accomplished by emptying its contents into the city streets, to be later washed away when it rained. In hotels or in residences of the wealthy, this task was performed by chamber maids, while the common man had to contend with his own shit! Also bear in mind that it was not until the early 1900s that the automobile began to replace the hundreds or even thousands of horses that also defecated at will and without reservation on those same streets. It was not until the late 1800s that the first sewer systems were built in Chicago and New York City. Until such time as the city sewers were built, the city streets doubled as open sewers. I believe it is no exaggeration to say that it is incomprehensible to imagine the foul stench of daily life in the great cities of that time.

To provide some context for this period in our history, I recall a weekend trip where I took my daughter to Springfield, Illinois, to see sights, such as the

LINCOLN'S HOME – This artist's depiction is an accurate representation of Lincoln's home in Springfield, IL, much as it was in his day and as it has been maintained and stands today.

Lincoln Library and museum, his law office, his tomb, and the state house where he served as a State Representative prior to becoming President. While Springfield is now a moderately sized modern city, many of the historical sites have been maintained much as they were in Lincoln's time. This was true for Lincoln's home, which we also toured.

While his home may at first glance appear somewhat upscale by even today's standards, for its time it was beyond the means of the vast majority. Although he came from a childhood that would be considered impoverished by most any standard, by the time he and his family resided at that house he was a very accomplished attorney, and although I hesitate to refer to him as wealthy, he was a man of significant financial means for his day. After touring much of the house, we came to a point where the tour guide asked if there were any questions. My daughter, I believe 8 years old at the time and too shy to ask for herself, looked to her father and asked, "Where is the potty?" This question was not for her own needs, but out of curiosity since over the course of the tour she noticed there was no bathroom in the house. Although I had some insights into what the answer to her question was, I in turn relayed her question to the tour guide. To my surprise he provided a fairly detailed answer, which came in several parts. First, he confirmed that the house had no bathroom; moreover, it had no plumbing other than a hand pump on the back porch that drew water from a well beneath it. When it came time to bathe, most likely every few weeks in the summer and every few months in the winter, they would place a metal tub on the back porch and fill it with water from the well that was first heated on the kitchen stove. The Lincoln family members would then take turns bathing, most likely sharing some, if not all, of the same bath water. If Mr. Lincoln or one of his sons needed to go potty, it was only a short walk out back to an outhouse, which was adjacent the stable where Mr. Lincoln's horse was kept. If Mrs. Lincoln needed to go potty, she most likely had a privy in her bedroom, which was described as a chair with a hole in it, beneath which was a chamber pot. When the privy was not in use, a seat cushion would disguise its true purpose. This was life behind the scenes for the man who would be our 16th president little more than 150 years ago and was representative, at least when it came to personal functions and hygiene, of life for most Americans for nearly another 100 years.

Much of the forgoing narrative relates to the advent of modern conveniences that came into existence only with the help of modern indoor/household plumbing systems, as well as municipal water distribution and sanitary sewerage systems. The earliest of these types of systems were first developed and put into widespread use nearly 2,000 years ago by the Roman Empire. While the aqueducts and public baths of Rome were indeed marvels in engineering for their time and made it possible for the city of Rome to grow to an estimated one million in population, they indeed fall far short of what we today would consider anywhere near acceptably tolerable. After the fall of Rome, municipal water distribution and sanitary sewerage systems did not reemerge until the late 1800s to early 1900s. For the thousands of years following the collapse of the Roman Empire until this period, sanitation and personal hygiene fell well short of what we would accept for our pets and/or farm animals. In the cities of the 1700s and 1800s, throughout the world, the outbreak of diseases, such as typhoid and cholera, ran rampant. The foul stench of open cesspools, common in urban life of the period, would have been intolerable to our modern senses.

The advent of municipal water supply and distribution systems came along nearly in parallel with, but somewhat in advance of, the sanitary sewers. This was a quite natural evolution, because while humans can (emphasis on the word "can") exist in close and continual proximity to raw sewage and waste, wells and in turn drinking water polluted by the open cesspools of the day were extremely deadly. The ready supply of water to fight fires in the cities, which were mostly constructed of wood, were also a higher priority than the human and animal waste in the streets. Water distribution systems of various forms and degrees of complexity were constructed in New York City as early as the Revolutionary War era, and have continuously evolved up to the present system, which came into existence in the early 1900s. As civilizations go, Americans readily take for granted the generally high quality of potable water supplied directly to their kitchen sinks. In fact, the tap water of today in New York City is some of the highest quality water attainable anywhere, and is, or at least should be, the envy of the world. With that said, some may point to the issues experienced in Flint, Michigan, in recent years. As unfortunate as the circumstances in Flint may be – and I mean not to minimize the situation (lead contamination of the public water supply) as it is indeed disastrous – it is also a fairly unique situation and an extreme exception to the norm.

While the earliest hot water systems may well also date back to the Romans and their public baths, any advances they made in this regard were also lost for centuries after the collapse of their empire. Throughout the ages, water was heated on an open fire, then in fireplaces, and later on the kitchen stove, much as the Lincolns had done. It may be obvious, but the advent of hot running water in the household would be dependent upon, and follow that of, municipal water distribution systems and household plumbing. Invention of the first commercially accepted and safe electric hot water heater (or automatic storage unit) is generally attributed to Edwin Ruud in 1889. So starting in the 1890s, if you had household plumbing and a tub, you could enjoy a hot bath without heating containers of water on the stove, but, although this may have been possible at that time, it was not until the mid-1900s that it became commonplace for most Americans. In my own lifetime, it was not until I was a teenager that I first experienced and enjoyed a hot shower. Until that time, it was bathing a few times a week in what I view today as an old-style cast-iron tub with its own legs and feet. Through the years, a shower has come to be a daily ritual and a perceived necessity for me, as I can only assume it has for most of you.

Since the discovery of fire and, more importantly, the ability to control it, estimated to be over a million years ago, mankind has relied upon it for the vast majority of this time in the form of open fires and torches as his sole source of warmth and light when neither was available from Mother Nature. Somewhere during this period, the first innovation came when humans ventured out of their caves and began building their own shelters, whereupon the first fireplaces came into existence. The open fireplace remained mankind's only source of warmth during long winter nights through the millennia with only marginal improvements in efficiency.

For all practical purposes, it was not until the Industrial Revolution and the manufacture of cast iron products that the first wood and coal burning stoves came into existence.. One of the most notable was the Franklin stove, which took its name from Benjamin Franklin, who invented it little more than 250 years ago. Stoves such as Franklin's, along with fireplaces, continued to provide the only source of heating homes in America and around the world for another 100 years or more. It was not until the early 1900s that central home heating began to become commonplace in America and other industrialized countries, and it was predominantly only found in regions where coal was a readily available source of fuel for these systems, which at their peak only heated about half of the homes in America. Of the balance of American homes, nearly half were still heated using wood as the source of fuel; the other half of these, or approximately 25% of all American homes, were without heat, predominately in more moderate climates in the South. For those of you not familiar with using coal as your source of heat, it needed much more attention than more modern oil, gas, or electric heating systems, for which about the only effort required is the adjustment and/or programing of a thermostat. Coal-fired heating systems required regular daily attention, which included shoveling the coal from the coal bin into the furnace, manually grating the ashes from the fire, and shoveling them into a pail for removal from the home. I personally know a little about this since in my youth it was one of my first chores, and few things were worse than allowing the fire to go out for lack of attention on a cold winter's night. Most of these coal systems were phased out and re-placed in the years following World War II, from the 1950s into the 1970s, with the oil, gas, or electric systems we have today.

Much like heating, fire in the form of open flame provided our only source of lighting throughout the millennia with little change. One of the few advancements, prior to the discovery of electricity and the electric light, was the oil lamp, fueled with olive oil in Roman times, although the oil lamp predates the Romans by considerable time, back even before the Egyptians. The candle is another whose history is somewhat parallel to that of the oil lamp although the origin of either is difficult, if not impossible, to pin down. Both the oil lamp and the candle have seen little change since their inception, other than their sources of fuel. For the candle it was the transition predominantly from beeswax to paraffin and stearin wax. For lamps it was predominantly the transition from vegetable-based oils to whale oil, then to petroleum-based oils. Few of these advancements made any appreciable improvements to the illumi-nation provided by either of these sources. Whale oil did however lead to a significant reduction in the world's whale population. The next real advancement was gas lighting, which provided for the lighting of public spaces in the 1800s and continued well into 1900s. While a significant advancement for society, especially for the city streets and public buildings of the day, it introduced an additional and increased potential for fire hazards to the many others that were already in abundance and of considerable, and very real, concern. Highly publicized in their time, fires in public theaters took countless lives at the turn of the century, one of which occurred in the town where I was raised, although well before my time. On January 13, 1908, 171 people perished in a fire that destroyed the Rhoads Opera House in Boyertown, Pennsylvania. The high loss of life in this fire was attributed to many things, such as poor egress to fire escapes and exits, doors that opened in rather than out, and the general panic that ensued. This was not unlike many similar tragedies of the day. However, in this case, the fire was attributed not to gas lighting but to a kerosene lamp being knocked over.

RHOADS OPERA HOUSE FIRE, BOYERTOWN, PA – Aftermath of the January 13, 1908 fire that claimed the lives of 171 attendees and people associated with the performance, as well as one firefighter.

Fortunately, through the efforts of men like Edison, Westinghouse, and Tesla, lighting from electricity came to us and was first displayed on a grand scale at the 1893 World's Fair in Chicago. From its early beginnings in the late 1800s, the vast infrastructure required to bring safe and reliable electricity to most Americans was constructed principally by private companies through the first half of the 1900s. Apart from the many other modern conveniences that electricity made possible, it was electric lighting that had the most profound impact on mankind. Without deliberating on any one of the specific items from what is indeed an exhaustive list, I believe this modern marvel can best be appreciated by considering that when the sun goes down virtually every aspect of your life is touched or made possible by electric lighting.

1893 WORLD'S FAIR, CHICAGO, IL – Also known as the "White City," it was the site of the largest scale exhibition of electrical lighting of its time. This was also the site where the Ferris wheel was first introduced.

Air conditioning is one of the many other modern conveniences brought to us only through the widespread, safe, reliable, and cheap availability of electricity. However, it is air conditioning that I believe is second only to the electric light in how profound a way it has affected humanity. As air conditioning found its way into the everyday lives of peoples throughout the world in the latter half of the 1900s, it made places on this good earth that were previously considered nearly inhospitable into a comfortable oasis and home to multitudes. Without air conditioning, Las Vegas today would be a ghost town in the middle of a dusty arid desert, known to nearly no one.

Since its founding by Ponce de Leon in 1513 up until the 1950s, Florida was considered by most to be a foreboding land of endless swamps and mosquitoes, little of which was inhabitable by civilized people due to the oppressive heat and humidity. Prior to the 1950s, Florida's population was less than 2.5 million for the entire state, which was less than a third of New York City's population at that time. In little more than half a century, it has now grown to more than 20 million, now exceeding that of the entire State of New York at this time. It's safe to say that without air conditioning there would be no Disney World, and Miami would still be inundated with alligators rather than cruise ships.

Until such time as mankind came to the domestication of wild animals, the only transportation available to him were his own two feet. Later with the invention of the wheel came the chariot, carriage, and horse-drawn cart, which made the transportation of goods for trade across land over most any distance reasonably viable. Through the millennia, the primary mode of transporting any significant quantity of goods for trade was limited to the world's oceans and natural waterways. Until the advent of steam power and in turn the railroad in the mid 1800s, these waterways were supplemented by manmade canals; the most notable and transformative of its time was the Erie Canal through upstate New York that went into operation in the early 1820s. Canal boats of the time were still powered by beasts of burden. In the case of the Erie Canal, they were drawn by horses and/or mules along the shoreline. In the latter half of the 1800s and into the early 1900s, many, if not most, of these canals were replaced by the railroads as the major form of transport for goods over land. Then in turn, these railroads lost their monopoly in transporting overland commerce to trucking with the invention and practical application of the internal combustion engine in cars and trucks, which also replaced the many horses and other beasts of burden from our cities, thereby improving sanitation in urban communities into the 1900s.

Although it was Henry Ford who made the automobile available to the masses in 1908, it was not until after World War II, in the 1950s, that it became commonplace in the lives of average Americans. Although the automobile was the principal contributor to the expansive growth of the city suburbs and made places accessible that previously were beyond the reach of most Americans, this mode of transportation was still quite primitive by today's standards. The interstate highway system was in its infancy in the late 1950s; in fact, one of its greatest proponents, President Eisenhower, experienced firsthand how torturous a cross-country excursion could be when in 1919 he was part of a military operation that took 62 days to move a mechanized army from Washington, DC, to San Francisco. Although it would take nearly another 35 years to complete the final legs of the Interstate Highway System as originally authorized, for at least the first half of this period the automobiles of that day had no air conditioning as they traveled across it. Those of us remaining who had experienced it know all too well how brutal those long summer vacation drives could be, especially those to Disney World in Florida or Disney Land in California. Ah yes, and that brings us to air travel. Although lost are the glamorous jet-setting days of the '60s and '70s, even with the tight seating, extensive security, and delays, cross-country and trans-Atlantic or trans-Pacific travel have never been so good!

Whether packing for a trip or simply deciding what to wear for the day, rarely is any thought given to the time when little or no thought was required. The clothing and fashion choices available to current generations are nearly endless and affordable to even those of limited means, and generally fit rather well. For nearly the first half of United States history, most of all clothing purchased by Americans came from England and/ or France. It was made to order, with fashion dominated by that which was being worn in the royal courts of Europe. But this was of course the case for only the limited few with the means to afford this indulgence. For the vast majority of Americans, the common working-class men and women of the day, clothing was made at home. Most of the common folk had only one or maybe two changes of everyday working clothing and one set of dress clothing, principally for Sunday church, special events, and holiday attire. One set of cloths would be allowed to air out, while the other was worn, and undergarments were essential to protect their clothing through the absorption of perspiration. Almost lost to us today, with the regular washing of clothing, is the concern of moths or other insects drawn to eat bacteria-laden clothing in storage. Children wore hand-me-downs from older siblings that was typically made of clothing cut down and modified for them from worn-out adult clothing. Most children went barefoot, as well as many adults, when the weather was accommodating.

By the latter half of the 1800s, with the introduction of the sewing machine and mechanized looms as part of the Industrial Revolution, the textile and garment industry began to develop in America, accelerating with the need for mass production of standardized uniforms for Civil War soldiers in the 1860s. Still, whether made at home or purchased, clothing was a major expenditure for Americans of the period, whether it be in the form of time and/or money. As the textile and garment manufacturing industry grew in conjunction with the introduction of department stores in the early 1900s, an affordable variety of fashion choices were made available to the masses, which continued to evolve and become ever more affordable and varied through that century.

1882 DE LONG EXPEDITION TO THE NORTH POLE – These men dressed in furs were the survivors of a 27-month odyssey across polar ice and frigid arctic seas. Twenty men of the original party of 33 perished after the sinking of the *Jeanette* and abandoning their search for a mythical warm-water polar sea.

The period from the late 1800s into the early 1900s was witness to some of the last great expeditions exploring the far reaches of our planet. When George Washington De Long set out for the North Pole in 1879 on board the USS *Jeannette* and later in 1914 when Sir. Ernest Shackleton set out for the South Pole on board the *Endurance*, neither had the benefit of Gore-Tex or other modern synthetics. They and their men's survival, in the most extreme of weather conditions (average winter temperatures as low as -30°F), was still dependent upon the natural fabrics of their day: cotton, wool, and animal skins/furs. Through their multi-year odysseys of survival, neither expedition reached its intended destination. Shackleton and the *Endurance*'s crew survived their ordeal, and while some of the crew of the *Jeanette* survived, De Long did not.

1914 SHACKLETON EXPEDITION TO THE SOUTH POLE – *Endurance* and her crew trapped in the ice pack. These men would go on to survive a harrowing 20-month journey of survival, dressed in the natural fabrics of their day, predominantly wool and cotton. They never got close to their goal of the South Pole, but they all survived.

The latter half of the 1900s saw the advent of new synthetic fabrics and a considerable decline in costs due to greater efficiency in the manufacturing processes. This brought with it a wide variety and abundance of clothing to the masses along with an evolutionary explosion in styles and fashion; the most significant and notable of which were for women. Most women likely dismiss any appreciation for, or give little thought to, the invention of the bra, or brassiere, which came into existence in the early 1860s, evolving through the early 1900s to closely resemble those worn today. Large scale commercial production in the 1930s made them affordable and available to the masses, replacing its predecessor, the corset. Any women who have a working knowledge of the corset will surely attest to their appreciation of the bra.

Ever give any thought to why women began wearing jeans, or, in general, pants, in the '60s? Was it the women's liberation movement? Although the timing was quite apropos, it was mostly coincidental. The truth is, it was for much more practical reasons, which have been well disguised. It was the sanitary pad or napkin and tampon that liberated the women of the 1960s. The first disposable pads came into being in the late 1800s and early 1900s, thought up by nurses on the battlefield looking for new methods to stop excessive bleeding. It took another fifty years for them to break through the taboos of the day and become affordable for the average woman. Until they were, women commonly employed the use of pieces of reusable padded cloth, or rags (hence the slang terminology). While we're on this subject, where would we be today without the disposable diaper, which coincidentally did not see common or widespread use until the 1960s? Before which, if you were not fortunate enough to afford a diaper service or a nanny, and not many were, the unpleasant and sometimes-foul task of changing a baby's diaper, multiple times a day, was compounded by disposing of its contents and laundering it to be recycled for its next use.

On May 13, 1775, the Second Continental Congress convened in Philadelphia, Pennsylvania, the largest and most affluent city of its day in the thirteen colonies. Here came together the upper echelon of society on the North American continent. This was a collection of the most respected, the most learned, the wealthiest merchants and great land holders of their time, and included names like George Washington, John Adams, Thomas Jefferson, Benjamin Franklin, and John Hancock. They arrived there by foot, on horseback, or by horse-drawn carriage, through city streets littered with human and animal excrement and other waste, having traveled days and even weeks from the far reaches of the thirteen colonies. It was a hot, sweltering, fly-infested summer, but because of the sensitive nature of their gathering and the deliberations that ensued, the doors and windows of the rooms in which they assembled were kept closed (and, need I remind you, there was no air conditioning). Even with the best personal hygiene of their day, the environment within those rooms must have been stifling to the senses. Yet through that long hot summer in Philadelphia, these men placed into jeopardy their lives and fortunes and, through their undertaking, put into motion a great struggle that yielded the liberties and prosperity that we enjoy today.

In Washington, DC, today, the politicians who occupy the halls of the great buildings made possible through the efforts of these men enjoy considerable comforts passed on to them only through the sacrifices of their predecessors. The pompous and quibbling politicians of today could learn much from these men regarding the priorities for their focus and attention. When we evaluate the average man's perceptions on the Necessities of Life in conjunction with their elite counterparts' platitudes on healthcare, what is more important to you? Who are they to now redefine basic human rights? The Founders intentionally laid a framework of broad freedoms, including property rights and the free exchange of goods and services. It has indeed served us well!

Chapter 2

Healthcare

"The art of medicine consists of amusing the patient while nature cures the disease."

—*Voltaire*

The year is 1793, and that summer in Philadelphia, the nation's capital at the time, over a third of the inhabitants are fleeing the city. Yellow Fever was ravaging the population, and members of the fledgling government, including George Washington, are fleeing alongside common citizens, not in search of "quality and/or affordable healthcare," but for their lives. By the time this outbreak is through, late that fall, more than 5,000 are dead (10% of the city's population). Although recorded as one of the worst outbreaks of the period, they were indeed fairly common most summers throughout the early years of our nation, hitting most of the major U.S. coastal cities and many others worldwide. The last major outbreak of Yellow Fever occurring in the United States was in New Orleans in 1905, wherein less than 500 had died, out of a population of approximately 300,000. Although considerably less than historical averages, it is a significant number by most any other measure, particularly when measured by today's standards.

But what was Yellow Fever, and why did it engender such fear among populations? The disease is transmitted by mosquitoes and believed to have originated in Africa, migrating to North America with the slave trade in the 1700s. Those infected by the disease initially exhibit symptoms similar to the flu, including fever, chills, loss of appetite, nausea and vomiting, headaches, fatigue, and muscle pain, which typically last about a week. When the symptoms of this phase of the disease subside, most recover; however, in about 15% of those infected, the disease enters a second, much more toxic phase. Those who enter this second phase continue with recurring fever, but this time accompanied by jaundice and abdominal pain from liver damage, bleeding from the mouth, eyes, and gastrointestinal tract causing blood-laden vomit. These symptoms may also be accompanied by kidney failure and delirium. The fatality rate of those infected through this second phase generally exceeds 5% and can reach as high as 50%. It was not until the late 1800s that the disease was found to be carried by mosquitoes. The virus was later isolated in the 1920s, with a vaccine subsequently being developed in the 1930s. Today the scourge of this virus is largely unknown to most populations of North America and the developed world; however, it remains to curse others, mostly in tropical areas of Africa and South America, annually infecting on average 200,000 people worldwide and leading to approximately 30,000 deaths.

Yellow Fever was by no means the only epidemic disease to ravage mankind through the course of history. The most recent and known to most of us today is the HIV/AIDS virus. Gaining much press in the 1980s and 1990s, although fading from public attention due to medical advances since that time, it has accounted for approximately 30 million deaths worldwide. As big a number as that may be, it falls well short of the death tolls and terror to befall mankind by some of the more notorious and many epidemic and pandemic diseases throughout history. The depth of the terror and horrors instilled in the people of their time are even more profound when compared to the much smaller population groups they afflicted of the period. Some of the more notable are summarized as follows:

Plague — Reoccurring throughout history but most notable, and likely the most devastating pandemic in human history, was an occurrence known as "the Black Death" affecting Europe, Asia, and North Africa in the years 1331 through 1353. During this occurrence alone the plague is attributed to having killed 75 to 200 million people, or 30% to 60% of these populations. It was first recorded to have reached the shores of Europe in 1347 when 12 merchant ships arrived at the Sicilian port of Messina. Upon meeting these ships at the docks, the people of Messina were horrified to find most of the sailors dead, and those who remained among the living were gravely ill with black boils covering their bodies, oozing blood and pus. From Messina the pestilence went on to ravage the rest of Europe for the next four to five years, during which time it reduced the populations of cities such as Florence, Paris, and London by more than half. It would take another 200 years for much of Europe to regain their pre-plague population numbers. In a time when nothing was known of the cause and/or spread of any disease, the horrific symptoms and mass casualties witnessed instilled a fear and terror that could only have been the worst wrath God could impose. The night skies were lit by bonfires, burning rotting corpses by the hundreds. By day, groups of people known as "flagellants" roamed from town to town, whipping themselves and each other into a frenzy with leather whips until they dripped with blood from their open wounds. As a tortured remnant of humanity, surviving children whose parents had succumbed to the curse are believed to have been the origin of the verse:

"Ring around the rosie, a pocket full of posies, ashes, ashes, we all fall down."

Smallpox — Regional outbreaks occurred regularly and, at times, in epidemic proportion throughout history. It is estimated that in 18th century Europe, with a fatality rate of 30%, smallpox claimed the lives of an estimated 400,000 people annually and left nearly a third of the infected survivors blind. In more recent years, with the increase in world population, it is estimated to have killed 500 million people in the last 100

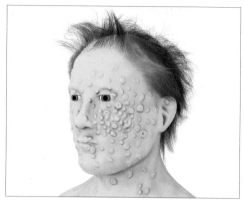

SMALLPOX – A scourge to all of mankind up until its eradication in the 1970's. For those that survived, the pustules caused by the disease left grotesque scaring. It is estimated to have killed as many as 500 million people in the last 100 years of its existence.

years of the disease's existence. Fortunately, this dreaded disease was eradicated in the late 1970s through a coordinated global immunization effort. Well before this pestilence was eliminated worldwide it was reasonably under control in much of the developed world through mass inoculations of the general public. As early as the Revolutionary War period in the United States, it was found that pus from the sores that covered the bodies of those infected could be used to inoculate others yet to be infected. In fact, due to early success with these methods, and so dreaded the disease, George Washington (who was immune after being infected as a youth) had his troops inoculated in this manner to avoid devastating outbreaks in the camps of his army.

Salmonella Enterica — This disease is believed to have been the principle killer that aided Spanish conquistador Hernando Cortes in his conquest of Mexico. At the time of his arrival to the New World in 1519, the Aztec civilization was estimated to have a population of about 25 million. After a series of epidemics in the decades that followed, those numbers plummeted to about one million. Before passing too severe a judgement on the Europeans for the demise of many native populations through the diseases that they brought with them to the New World, in balance, consider that these same early explorers brought syphilis back to Europe from the native populations of the New World. Although not as deadly as the diseases they traded in this exchange, syphilis, until the advent of antibiotics, was a scourge like few others and had a significantly adverse social impact on European society.

Measles — Regional outbreaks occurred regularly throughout history, and although its fatality rate is significantly less than many of the other diseases cited here (less than 1% but up to 10% in malnourished populations), this disease had historically been very prevalent throughout the world with children under the age of 15 being its primary victims. Due to the regular and common frequency of outbreaks throughout history, the butcher's toll for this disease is difficult to estimate. Although still prevalent today in some third world areas, it has been nearly eradicated within the United States and most other portions of the developed world through immunization. Out of sight and out of mind for decades in most of these areas, it has now gained increased media attention in recent years due to regionalized outbreaks in the United States. The proliferation of misinformation about vaccines and ignorance about the lethality of such diseases has led to a subsequent increase of people electing not to have themselves and/or their children inoculated. This reduction in "herd immunity" has unfortunately resulted in the reemergence of this disease in pockets of the population.

Malaria — The scourge of this disease has besieged mankind throughout recorded history and is still with us today. Although generally well controlled in most developed societies today, consequently falling from public consciousness in these same societies, it is still a curse for many impoverished peoples living in tropical climates. Similar to yellow fever, this disease is transmitted by mosquitoes and exhibits many of the same flu-like symptoms. However, unlike yellow fever, there are no vaccines to inoculate against the disease. Most of the success against the spread of this disease has been achieved through mosquito control measures, such as insecticides, and the elimination of standing water, which is required for the pests to propagate. There are also several modern medications available to protect against the disease, but there are growing concerns over the possibilities of resistance developing in the parasites against some of these pharmaceuticals. Still widespread in the tropics, there are hundreds of millions of cases recorded each year, with approximately a half million of those cases resulting in death. The death toll of malaria over the course of history, prior to modern medical advancements, is unknown and likely incalculable.

Influenza — This disease has reoccurred throughout history, with the most recent and notable pandemic, known as "the Spanish flu," spreading worldwide in the years 1918 through 1920. During this period of time, it killed an estimated 75 million people or nearly double the total death toll of the first World War. This is presumably a contributing factor in ending that war. The influenza virus (the flu or common cold), which remains with us today, is nowhere near the killer it once was. Although there is no cure, primarily due to the multitude of strains and variations through mutation, it is readily controlled through vaccines, and symptoms are mitigated with other modern medications. There are, however, concerns for the potential mutation of a resistant strain that could lead to a future pandemic, similar to or worse than the Spanish flu.

Typhus — Symptoms of this disease include fever, red spots over the arms, back, and chest, attention deficit leading to delirium, and gangrenous sores giving off the smell of rotting flesh. This disease is recorded in history as early as the 1400s and has afflicted human societies with increasing virulence through the years as these societies grew in population density. Spread by biting insects, principally fleas carried by rats, the proliferation of this petulance is associated with the growth of population centers lacking in sanitation. Its decline in the developed world was a result of public sanitation in communities in the late 1800s and early 1900s. Still today typhus is found in most third world nations; however outbreaks have occurred in recent years in Los Angeles primarily affecting, and a result of, a growing homeless population.

Cholera — Similar to typhus, this disease is associated with the lack of or poor sanitation and has seen a historical parallel in the increase of outbreaks with the growth in population densities coupled with extremely poor sanitary conditions. Unlike typhus, this disease is a bacterial infection of the small intestine caused by unsafe water and food contaminated by human feces containing the bacteria. Infection by cholera causes vomiting and muscle cramps but is most noted for the severe watery diarrhea lasting for days and causing extreme dehydration.

Dysentery — This is an inflammatory disease of the intestine, including the colon, resulting in severe diarrhea. It's caused by several types of infectious pathogens, including bacteria, viruses and parasites, which are usually introduced orally through the ingestion of contaminated food or water. Today dysentery is generally uncommon in the developed world, and even if contracted it's rarely fatal with symptoms lasting less than a week. However, in the third world and for most of history it can be and has been a deadly killer, principally being fatal for the malnourished.

While diarrhea is very unpleasant under any circumstance, in the case of dysentery, we're are speaking of significant and sometimes violent watery discharges, causing extreme dehydration. It may be difficult to comprehend today in the developed world, but dehydration to this degree can be very lethal, particularly for the very young and those already lacking in nourishment and/or sanitary conditions.

Although not of the epidemic or pandemic proportions of those previously cited, there are a few others worthy of note that have afflicted mankind through the millennia, some of which have been conquered, or at least controlled, by modern medicine in recent decades. Similar to the above, the torment and agony these once caused humanity has now all but faded from our modern consciousness. Some of the more prominent include:

Polio — Best known for its affliction of Franklin Delano Roosevelt (FDR), the 32nd President of the United States and the only President to require the use of a wheelchair. While this disease has a fatality rate in no way comparable to those noted above, it was little less feared due to its regular outbreaks most summers, the fact that it predominantly attacked young children, and its horrific symptoms, such as muscle weakness/fatigue. One side effect of this disease had the potential of leading to difficulties in breathing and paralysis, in some cases, such as FDR's, for life. This disease is spread through water and food contaminated by human feces containing the viruses and is readily communicable from infected people to the uninfected, even when symptoms are not present. It was polio that brought a device called the "iron lung" into prominence in the 1930s, bringing some comfort to those with severe breathing difficulties and saving many from death due to respiratory failure. Polio started to come under control with better sanitation in the early 1900s and, finally, with the development of a vaccine in 1950. It then faded from prominence in the decades that followed shortly thereafter. Although outbreaks still occur in parts of the world, it was declared eradicated in the United States in 1994.

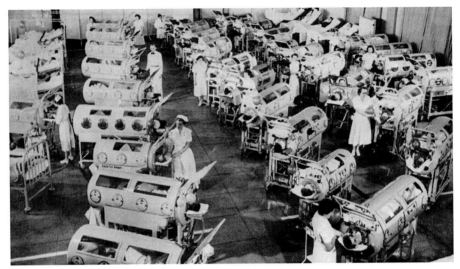

1950s POLIO WARD – Iron lungs as pictured here brought relief to those having difficulty breathing from the disease and saved many a life in the early to mid 1900s.

Tuberculosis (TB) — Known to prior generations as consumption, due to its most notable symptom of significant weight loss, this disease has been with mankind since antiquity and is still with us today predominately in the developing world. With the advent of antibiotics and vaccines in the mid 1900s, it had been effectively driven from the continents of North America, Europe, and Australia. However, drug resistant strains emerged in the 1980s that all but eliminated any hope of completely eradicating TB worldwide. Although nearly out of sight and out of mind for the vast majority of these populations, today it is estimated that nearly 25% of the populations of South America, Africa, and Asia are infected with TB, resulting in an estimated 1.6 million deaths in 2017. TB is a respiratory affliction, which in addition to the symptom of severe weight loss those actively infected suffer from fever and a chronic cough, including coughing up blood or bloodstained mucus. Due to the nature of these symptoms TB is readily communicable via the cough of those infected and was therefore rampantly spread with the increase of population densities in cities from the 1600s through the early 1900s. For the same reasoning, it was also a scourge to armies where troops were gathered in large groups or encampments and family unites or any groups in close proximity. Folklore from these earlier times associated TB with vampires because when the first member of a family died of the disease, exhibiting extreme weight loss and resembling their vision of a vampire, other family members would succumb to the disease shortly thereafter.

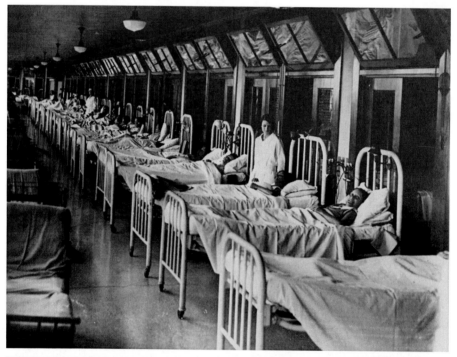

WAVERLY HILLS SANATORIUM, LOUISVILLE, KENTUCKY – Opening in 1910 to house 40 to 50 tuberculosis patients, it grew to treat more than 400 at its peak. It closed in 1961. Today it is mostly known as a paranormal attraction. *Reprinted with the permission of* The (Louisville) Currier Journal.

Up to the 1800s, it is estimated that TB had killed one in seven of all the people that had ever lived. By the mid 1800s some of the earliest success in at least curtailing the spread of the disease was achieved through the quarantine or isolation of those afflicted, thus spawning the "sanitarium movement." Sanitariums were promoted as not just a means to spare the healthy, but also to heal the sick. At their peak in the mid 1900s there were over 800 such institutions providing accommodations for more than 125,000 patients. Within only a few decades after the peak of these institutions, they were all but gone as a result of advancements in modern medicine over the same period.

Infection — Thankfully, due to antibiotics, we view infection today mostly as little more than a nuisance. Understand that I am referring here to the general public; on the contrary, hospitals and healthcare professionals are acutely aware of the dangers that infection carries with it. Prior to the mid 1900s, attitudes toward infection were quite different and anything but cavalier. Before antibiotics and the basic understanding we have today with respect to personal hygiene and the need to clean and sanitize open wounds, this was a deadly and very common killer. In fact, minor wounds as simple and common as a skinned knee or a splinter could be fatal if infection set in. In war, if one was not fortunate enough to be killed outright in battle, there was a good probability of a slow and agonizing death from even the most minor of battlefield wounds. While this was a reality throughout the history of human conflict, it was vividly experienced, witnessed, and recorded by many during the American Civil War, which was the last large-scale conflict fought prior to knowledge of the relationship between germs and infection. Of the more than 600,000 deaths of combatants during this conflict, it is estimated that as many as two thirds were the result of infectious diseases. This was at a time when the population of the

United States (both North and South) was approximately 31 million. A good portion of these deaths were the result of infectious diseases such as typhus, cholera, dysentery, and salmonella (food poisoning), but the butcher's toll through the infection of battlefield wounds was the curse of any wounded soldier.

From ancient times the belief, which still prevailed through the Civil War, was that the white creamy discharge, or laudable pus, that oozed from infected wounds was a normal part of the healing process. A discolored, often blood-tinged, watery discharge accompanied by a foul smell was called "malignant pus" and was a sign that a secondary infection had set in. Four forms of deadly infectious wounds were recognized during the Civil War — all of which were agonizingly painful and had mortality rates of 40% to 90%. They were identified as tetanus, erysipelas, gangrene, and pyemia (blood poisoning). Tetanus affected the nervous system via toxins produced by the bacteria, causing painful muscle spasms typically in the neck and jaw, hence the term lockjaw. These spasms were often so severe, they distorted the body and even broke bones. Erysipelas gradually ate away flesh, resulting in grotesquely swollen, discolored, and painful limbs. Gangrene caused tissue in the wounds to die and blacken quickly, spreading at a rate of half an inch in just an hour or more. Tissue destroying infections eroded blood vessels that would hemorrhage and rapidly kill patients. Pyemia was the spread of bacteria from infection via the blood stream throughout the body, causing abscesses, which if formed in the brain or heart could kill suddenly. As it would spread up through a limb it was identifiable by red streaked and swollen blood vessels. These infections were typically treated by burning the infected tissue or amputation of the infected limbs, which often served little more than to prolong the agony.

Venereal Disease — Although there are more than 30 types of sexually transmitted disease (STD) or venereal disease, the focus here is on the more historically significant and well-known syphilis and gonorrhea. Besides the grotesque symptoms of these diseases, which include pus-like discharges, painful urination, open sores or chancres, rashes covering most of the body, and wart-like sores in the mouth or genital areas, they can cause damage to the brain and nervous system and damage to the cardiovascular system, liver, bones, and joints. A unique aspect of these diseases is that, without antibiotics, once contracted they are with you for life, leading to long-term abnormalities, such as infertility, complications in childbirth (including passing the disease to your offspring), dementia, and blindness, if you are unfortunate enough that they don't simply kill you. As you can imagine these diseases were a social scourge for the majority of mankind's history, during which time the only thing that stood between widespread epidemic and pandemic outbreaks were the cultural mores of a given society. For these two, as well as several other venereal diseases, the invention of penicillin in the mid 1900s was found to be a cure, thus bringing its proliferation in the developed world under control if not to their end.

You may have noted one recurrent aspect of the majority of the pestilence summarized above, that being their common demise in or about the early to mid-1900s. As you may have also noted, there were two major breakthroughs during that short period: first the improvement in personal hygiene and general sanitary conditions and second the invention of antibiotics and vaccines. The combined effect was a monumental transformation in humanity, as if moving from a perpetual darkness into light. Although there are other contributing factors, average life expectancy and child mortality rates are generally good and accepted measures of healthcare. A quick look at world data for each yields near parallel observations.

Average Life Expectancy:

❖ From antiquity up to 1900, rarely exceeding 30 years of age.

❖ In 1900, less than 40 years of age.

❖ In the mid-1900s, it was nearly 50 years of age.

❖ In the 2000s, it now exceeds 70 years of age.

Child Mortality Rates:

❖ From antiquity up to 1900, as high as 50%.

❖ In 1900, it exceeded 35%.

❖ In the mid-1900s, it was near 20%.

❖ In the 2000s, it is now less than 4.5%.

Somewhat related to this topic is the advent of modern birth control. While protracted debate could ensue over this topic falling under the heading of "Healthcare," I will refrain from any moral discussion, simply stating that in today's society it is viewed in this context. Nonetheless it is surely related, and has had a profound effect on our society since the 1960s. Although forms of birth control have existed since before the days of the Romans, prior to the 1900s it had little relevance for societies as a form of family planning due to the high infant and child mortality rates of the time. During these years its greatest value, apart from reducing the spread of disease, was for the lives of individual women who faced the potentially fatal consequences of complications arising from childbirth. Data on the subject of maternal mortality in antiquity is sketchy, and even in recent centuries there are significant variations in the data, but in general in the early 1900s, roughly 400 out of 100,000 women died from complications in childbirth, which has today dropped to about 15 out of 100,000.

At first glance some may be suspect of the above data based upon preconceived generalizations, specifically with respect to average life expectancy through the ages. Certainly, we are familiar with famous people from history, nearly all of whom lived well beyond the numbers presented above. For instance, we are generally all well aware of Benjamin Franklin and have our own mental images of him being the great wise old statesman among our Founding Fathers. In fact, he did indeed live to the ripe old age 84. John Adams and Thomas Jefferson, the second and third Presidents of the United States, lived to the ages of 90 and 83 years respectively, both passing on the exact same day, July 4, 1826, exactly fifty years from the date of the Declaration they had both put their hands to and later signed. And surely there are many others, dating farther back in history, but they are an aberration from the norm. The famous people we have learned about and recall from history are truly the one-percenters. The masses who lived and died in obscurity were ravaged by the pestilence outlined above. Often malnourished, poorly clothed, and living in extremely unsanitary conditions, they were easy prey for the Grim Reaper.

Even many of the upper echelon of society were not immune to the scourge of prolific disease that came in many forms and was always a near and present danger. Being born to aristocracy and the lifestyle it afforded was by no means any assurance of surviving to prominence, and, the nature of recorded history as it is, if you don't live long enough to make a name for yourself, there's little chance to have your name recorded in the history books. Even George Washington, who was noted to be a remarkable physical specimen for his day, died at the age of 67, much earlier than many of his contemporaries of the founding class. Due to his prominence, much is known about the life of George Washington, who eluded the clutches of death many times over the course of his life, from diseases such as smallpox, which he contracted in his youth, to the many risks he took in battle and his many resultant near death encounters. Whether it was good fortune, sheer luck, or divine providence, he did live to become one of the most prominent figures in all of history. Ironically, in the end it was nothing more than the common cold that took his life on December 14, 1799. However, his untimely death was just as likely brought on by the medical treatment he received (bloodletting by his physician) as opposed to the virus itself.

At the time of his death, George Washington had only one of his original teeth remaining. Although well known for his overall remarkably impressive physical condition, his ability as a great horsemen in his day, and the great admiration he received from ladies, he suffered all through his life from bad and failing teeth. Contrary to popular belief, he did not have wooden teeth. He wore dentures, most likely made from teeth extracted from human and/or animal corpuses, which in their day were generally ill fitting and very uncomfortable to say the least. Information on the quality of oral health through history is somewhat mixed, but it is generally believed that dental problems afflicted the upper classes to a much greater degree due to their ability to afford and consume foods, such as sugar, which promote dental decay. The professional practice of dentistry did not begin to emerge until the late 1800s and early 1900s, at least in a form that we would recognize today. Up until that time the only way to deal with a toothache was to have it pulled, which in the days prior to the dentist or in rural areas was generally performed by the village blacksmith or barber.

One final measure of general health that can't be overlooked is the world's population recorded and estimated through history. Based upon the foregoing information provided in this chapter the data summarized as follows should come as little surprise.

❖ From 10000 BC up to 5000 BC, estimated to be less than 5 million.

❖ From 5000 BC up to 1 AD, increased to about 200 million.

❖ From 1 AD up to 1000 AD, increased to about 250 million.

❖ From 1000 AD up to 1500 AD, increased to about 500 million.

❖ From 1500 AD up to 1800 AD, increased to about 1.0 billion.

❖ From 1800 AD up to 1900 AD, increased to about 1.5 billion.

❖ From 1900 AD up to 1950 AD, increased to about 2.5 billion.

❖ From 1950 AD up to 2000 AD, increased to about 8.0 billion.

At this point it should now be readily evident that the current state of public health far exceeds that of any other period in history, and by considerable measure in the developed world, especially in the United States. The issue of "Healthcare" being so prominent today is in reality a focus on the cost of health insurance, which should be directed simply toward the underlying costs of healthcare. But then this is a much more difficult challenge, and one that politicians doggedly avoid. With the technological innovations of recent decades, we have seen considerable increases in costs, with only marginal gains in improved health and longevity. Are we now the victims of our own success? In the United States those 65 years of age and older represent 16% of the population but account for 36% of the healthcare spending.

Postscript: At the time I arrived at the final editing of my manuscript for this work, the coronavirus, or COVID-19, had grown to be a global pandemic. As of this writing it is beginning to appear that in the U.S. and worldwide the rate of spread of this contagion may be approaching its peak. Although it is extremely difficult to anticipate the final tallies of those infected and dead as a result of this epidemic, even for the professionals, surely the number of people infected will be measured in the millions (U.S.) or tens of millions (worldwide), and the dead in the hundreds of thousands (U.S.) or millions (worldwide). While these numbers are well short of the historical scourges cited above, particularly when evaluated as a function of world populations in their time, it is imposing other significant and extreme impacts in the lives of people worldwide, not just in the way they live their daily lives and the heightened anxiety over an unknown future, but to their livelihood and financial wellbeing. How it will ultimately play out in the economies of the United States and the world is anyone's guess, and at this time it appears that economists everywhere are indeed merely guessing. If nothing else, at least this virus might give current generations a sense of, or greater appreciation for, the hardships preceding generations had to endure and overcome. However, flu-like symptoms and difficulty breathing, in some cases requiring the aid of a ventilator (less than 1%), give rise to nowhere near the psychological impact that vomiting bile and/or blood or suffering from pustules on the skin that oozed pus and blood had on past victims and survivors alike.

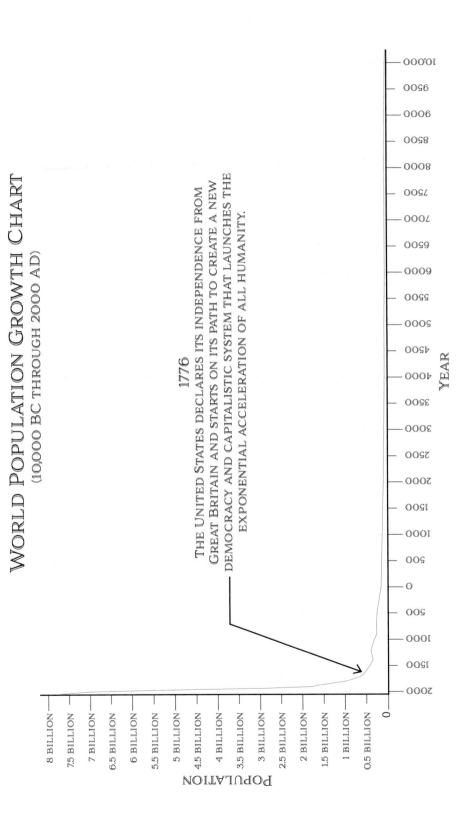

WORLD POPULATION GROWTH CHART
(10,000 BC THROUGH 2000 AD)

1776

THE UNITED STATES DECLARES ITS INDEPENDENCE FROM GREAT BRITAIN AND STARTS ON ITS PATH TO CREATE A NEW DEMOCRACY AND CAPITALISTIC SYSTEM THAT LAUNCHES THE EXPONENTIAL ACCELERATION OF ALL HUMANITY.

YEAR

POPULATION

Chapter 3

War and Conflict

"Never in the field of human conflict was so much owed by so many to so few."

—*Winston Churchill*

Few things have been with mankind so consistently and have impacted so many people as war has. It has consumed not just the lives of multitudes, but huge swaths of our collective innovation, efforts, and output. Ever since the first man coveted the property of another, conflict between the two had evolved into warring factions of aggressors and defenders. The pages of the Bible, particularly the Old Testament, and other works from antiquity are stained with a preoccupation about the conflicts of men and their wars. At the time of the founding of the United States this preoccupation was recorded in the writings of Madison, Hamilton, and Jay in *The Federalists*. A considerable portion, if not a majority of the 85 volumes, focused an emphasis, if not a fixation, on their concerns toward the potential conflicts of interest and the ensuing potential for war with the European powers, being drawn into war between these powers, war with the indigenous tribes of savages, as well as war between the states of the proposed union. In retrospect we may well look back in admiration as to how prophetic and how appropriately placed this preoccupation indeed was.

Notwithstanding some of the great wars of very ancient times, much of the earliest terrors of human conflict came from what we today collectively term as the barbarians, generally perceived to be primitive, uncivilized tribal groups of intensely brutal, cruel, and warlike marauders raiding villages on their quest to rape, pillage, and plunder their victims. In a time where your mere existence and struggle for survival was dependent upon the toil of hard daily labor, try to imagine, if you can, the incessant fear harbored for your life and the lives of those you love from this threat. At any moment, on any given day, you and your village could be overrun by any variety of unknown miscreant wretches, burning your home, raping your woman and daughters, seizing your harvest and livestock, and hacking you and your sons to death with their blades. In a world with little order, this was as much a part of life as it surely was of death. Even with the relative order brought to an uncivilized world by the Roman Empire, the threat was omnipresent. While Rome did bring some measure of civility to an extremely barbarous time, it brought with it, with their legions, their own form of brutality by the sword to neighboring civilizations on their quest to conquer the ancient world. The Roman Empire was, amongst other things, principally a society that was both politically and economically based upon war and conquest. The Punic Wars alone, which consisted of three major engagements, are estimated to have resulted in a death toll of over one million, and this was at a time when the population of the Roman Empire was about 50 million.

During its approximate 1,000-year existence, the Roman Empire did bring significant technological advances and improvements in the general wellbeing of many of its citizens, including an increase in life expectancy, but then all of this was relative to the context of the extreme disarray and brutality of prior periods. For most all of the history of

Rome, it was almost continually at war in one form or another with the exception of the so-called Pax Romana, or Roman Peace, lasting from 27 BC to 180 AD, but, of course, this too was relative to the scale of Roman war during the balance of time. When it comes down to attempting to quantify the toll of all these wars with an estimated body count, the accuracy of much of the historical data is suspect, and estimates are widely varied and debated. However, it is not hard to speculate at a number exceeding 10 million. In war with Rome, there was no question that to the victor went the spoils. Depending upon the resistance put forth against a Roman campaign, the only alternative to death was slavery. It is estimated that 30% of the populace of Rome comprised slaves. Control of such a large portion of the population in bondage presented Rome with additional internal difficulties in maintaining the peace. As a result, there were several major slave rebellions, one of which grew to a magnitude that potentially threatened the empire. In 73 BC a slave revolt began with the escape of about 70 slave-gladiators from a gladiator school in Capua. Over a two-year period of raiding estates and villages across the Roman countryside, they grew to number 120,000 liberated slaves, including women and children. Having defended themselves and defeating the Roman military in several engagements during this time, the rebellion was finally put down in 71 BC. Of the combatant slaves, more than 30,000 were killed in the final engagements, and 6,000 who were captured were made an example of by being crucified along the Appian Way from Capua to Rome. Their corpses were left to hang there, to be picked apart by scavenging birds, and to rot in the Mediterranean sun as a warning to other slaves who might consider another such insurrection. It was this uprising that put the name Spartacus in our history books, and, while this revolt is widely known because of Hollywood productions portraying the conflict, it is by no means the only or first major slave rebellion of its kind that Rome had to contend with.

The First Servile War occurred in Sicily, taking place in the years 135 through 132 BC. The Second Servile War, also occurring in Sicily, took place in the years 104 through 100 BC. Both enveloped the entire island of Sicily, terrorizing and taking the lives of many of the land-holding class on the island and cutting the Roman Republic off from a major source of the grain that fed its people. In the end, it the barbarians are believed to have been a major contributing factor in the ultimate fall of the Roman Empire some 500 years later.

After the fall of Rome, urban life began to dissolve and fell once again into a period of intellectual darkness and barbarity, this time lasting about 500 years and known as the Dark Ages. Although not of the scale of Roman engagements, this period was also marked by frequent war-fare brought to Europe by warring and cold-blooded marauders, such as the Huns, the Goths, and the Vandals. At the later portion of this period, as European societies began to reemerge and make way for the Renaissance, Europe was antagonized by yet another band of godless pagans, referred to as the Vikings. These seafaring invaders principally harassed coastal areas of England and the northern coast of Europe. For this period of history, fraught with brutality, the reputation of and the fear instilled by the Vikings was unparalleled. In addition to the death and destruction brought on by their raids, they were known to abduct the women of the communities they prayed upon, taking them back on their ships to Scandinavia. It is believed that these women were taken to supplement a shortage of Viking women, most likely due to selective infanticide of female children in preference of male offspring.

This prolonged period of dismal existence and marauding barbarians in Europe transitioned into the Renaissance. Although this terminology may garner visions of blossoming cultural, artistic, and intellectual pursuits, it continued to see the bloodshed of warring factions on a regular and grand scale in the years that followed. Warring factions emerged as urban communities grew into city-states and later monarchal nations. Some of the more notable conflicts of this period, for both their historical significance, as well as the carnage they wrought are summarized as follows:

❖ The Crusades (1095-1291) — 1 to 3 million estimated deaths

❖ Mongol Conquests (1206-1368) — 30 to 40 million estimated deaths

❖ Hundred Years War (1337-1453) — 2.5 to 3.5 million estimated deaths

❖ War of the Roses (1455-1487) — 35,000 to 50,000 estimated deaths

❖ French Wars of Religion (1562-1598) — 2 to 4 million estimated deaths

❖ Thirty Years War (1618-1648) — 3 to 11.5 million estimated deaths

❖ Seven Years War (1756-1763) — 1 to 1.5 million estimated deaths

❖ Napoleonic Wars (1803-1815) — 3.5 to 7 million estimated deaths

Historical records for these periods, although more reliable than earlier periods, also leave much to be desired, hence their presentation as an estimated range. Irrespective, when compared to the estimated population of 50 million to 100 million for Europe during the same period (1000 through 1800) the general magnitude of the carnage brought by these conflicts is plainly evident. The later part of this period also saw the discovery of the New World, which was not without its own internal warring factions. Well before the early explorers and the conquistadors who followed the discovery of the New World in 1492, the indigenous peoples of the Western Hemisphere, contrary to the myth of the "noble savage," practiced their own forms of brutality between warring tribes and within their own great civilizations. However, when faced with the technology and disease brought to the New World by the Europeans, they were no match in the end. It is estimated that the Spanish conquest of the Aztec Empire resulted in more than 24 million fatalities alone.

The intense horrors and terror brought to the people of these periods by the near continual brutality of the conflicts of their time are difficult, if not impossible, for us to comprehend today. However, evidence of it is with us today in the form of the many great structures and fortifications that have survived the millennia. Nearly thirty years ago I first traveled to Puerto Rico and saw for the first time a walled city by the name of Old San Juan. I have traveled back to Puerto Rico several times since, and the awe originally induced by what I saw only intensifies with each successive visit. Each time I explore more and more of the expansive ramparts, increasing my understanding of the scope and extent of these massive fortifications, which were built over a 200-year period, from the early 1500s to the late 1700s. There are towering walls, some exceeding 40 feet in height, enormous gates, gigantic ramps for cannon, and a collective of other massive defensive fortifications. However, with the more I have seen and learned, quite ironically, the more difficult it is for me to comprehend the full scope of these grand and mighty works. Most difficult for me to make sense of is understanding the motivation to exert and bring to bear the resources and efforts necessary to build such colossal structures.

EL MORRO – This old Spanish structure guarded the entry to the port of San Juan in Puerto Rico. It is part of other fortifications that surrounded and guarded the City of Old San Juan. Today it greets the almost daily passage of cruise ships visiting that city.

All around the world we see great cathedrals and other great temples and monuments, which cause pause and amazement for their sheer size and complexity, particularly when viewed in the context of the periods in time and the conditions under which they were constructed. Clearly the common and readily understood motivating factor for the construction of these shrines is the worship and devotion to an all-powerful deity. The structures surrounding Old San Juan are very different and born of fear. Bear in mind, these structures were constructed in a time where access alone to Caribbean islands, such as Puerto Rico, was by sailing ships, requiring harrowing voyages that took weeks or even months. In this context and based upon the enormity of the structures, the fear harbored by the inhabitants and those who built these fortifications must have had an intensity beyond my comprehension.

In 1776, thirteen colonies on the North American continent declared their independence from Great Britain. The six-year struggle that followed came to be known as the American Revolution. However, this revolution was unlike most of revolutions that played out over the course of history. It was indeed unique in many ways. First, although the colonies ultimately won their independence, they did not overthrow the King of England. More important is that at the conclusion of this conflict, a new nation was formed without devolving into a period of anarchy and factional conflicts for power. As this new nation was finding its way, in Europe the French Revolution was taking place and playing out quite differently. During the French Revolution, 1793 saw the start of a period known as the "Terror." Lasting little more than a year, by its end some 17,000 were officially sentenced to death and publicly executed by beheading. It was during this period that the guillotine also took the heads of both King Louis XVI and his wife, Marie Antoinette. This terror would later be eclipsed by two other revolutions more than a hundred years later. Both the Bolshevik Revolution in Russia and the Communist Revolution in China claimed lives in the millions.

From before the founding of the United States, the miseries of war have continued with us from early incursions with the native inhabitants and European conflicts, which were also fought on the North American continent — such as the French and Indian war, the war for independence against the British Empire, and the war of 1812, etc. — but none of these can hold a candle to the wrath brought upon the people of the United States as that of the American Civil War. The enormity of the devastation and bloodletting during this conflict is unparalleled in the gruesome slaughter and destruction brought on by a war that marked the transition of ancient warfare to what we refer to as modern warfare. If God himself were seeking atonement for the original sin of slavery it would be difficult to think of Him conceiving a more horrific meat grinder. The Civil War brought with it from years past the butchery of weapons, such as the sword and bayonet, adding much improved ballistics and lethality to the rifle and artillery, as well as the introduction of the first machine-gun — named for its inventor Richard J. Gatling. At a time when the population of the United States was little more that 30 million, nearly 650,000 perished, or roughly more than 2% of the combined population of both the North and South. Another 450,000 are estimated to have been wounded, many of whom suffered grotesque scarring, disfigurement, and amputation. In summary, it is estimated that one in five of those who fought in that war died. As great a toll as this was, the mass bloodshed that took place during individual engagements was staggering and unprecedented.

❖ Vicksburg — approximately 37,000 casualties over 48 days

❖ 2nd Manassas — approximately 22,000 casualties over 3 days

❖ Antietam — approximately 23,000 casualties over 3 days

❖ Stones River — approximately 24,500 casualties over 3 days

❖ Shiloh — approximately 23,500 casualties over 2 days

❖ Chancellorsville — approximately 31,000 casualties over 7 days

❖ The Wilderness — approximately 30,000 casualties over 3 days

❖ Spotsylvania — approximately 30,000 casualties over 14 days

❖ Chickamauga — approximately 34,500 casualties over 3 days

❖ Gettysburg — approximately 51,000 casualties over 3 days

From the above summary, it may well be difficult to grasp the magnitude of the mass carnage wrought in the battles that took place during this conflict. The Battle of Antietam saw the highest single-day death toll in American history. By the end of the day on September 17, 1862, more than 22,000 lay dead, wounded, or missing. At Cold Harbor, an estimated 7,000 Union soldiers were killed and thousands more wounded in just 20 minutes of fighting. At Shiloh, during heavy overnight rains, surviving soldiers heard the sounds of feral pigs scavenging and eating the dead remains of their fallen countrymen left behind in the mud. During the Wilderness campaign, wounded and dying soldiers were known to have been burned alive by brush fires that started during the conflict. At the Battle of Gettysburg, the total casualties from the three-day engagement claimed more than the entirety of the Revolutionary War and the War of 1812 combined. In addition to the men killed at Gettysburg, it is estimated that nearly 5,000 horses and mules also perished during the incursion. At Gettysburg, as at many other battlefields during the war, dead men and horses would lay where they fell for days until they were eventually buried, nearly 40% of which were never identified. And during campaigns later in the war, combatants would come across the skulls and skeletal remains of unburied soldiers lost during earlier incursions.

The Civil War also took a brutal toll on the civilian population, particularly in the South where the majority of the battles were fought. In later years of the conflict, with the Confederate economy collapsing and much of the infrastructure destroyed, the civilian populace was besieged by rampant starvation and disease. It is estimated that approximately 50,000 civilians died during the war. With nearly all the men of the Southern states serving in the military during the conflict, women and children were left to fend for themselves. Armies of both the North and the South, measuring in the tens of thousands, would forage the countryside seizing food and livestock to sustain their ranks, thereby depriving local inhabitants of the necessities required for their own survival. Northern armies would burn to the ground and destroy anything remaining that they perceived could support the Confederate war effort. Great urban centers, such as Atlanta, Georgia; Richmond, Virginia; Columbia, South Carolina; and Fredericksburg, Virginia, were destroyed; if they were not destroyed by artillery and the fires that ensued, they were torched by their own retreating armies.

RICHMOND, VA (POST CIVIL WAR) – Ruins of the city after its capture by Ulysses S. Grant in his pursuit of Lee's Army of Northern Virginia.

CHARLESTON, SC (POST CIVIL WAR) – Ruins of the city after its capture by William T. Sherman during his march through the South to the sea.

Although the South fared far worse in this conflict, Northern civilians were certainly not immune to the grisly and gruesome horrors of a war that became all too common among the Southern populace. In the summer of 1863, two great armies converged on the small town of Gettysburg, Pennsylvania. Having a population of less than 2,500 at the time, Gettysburg would be witness to one of the world's greatest military confrontations, and certainly the greatest in American history. At the crossroads of Gettysburg, a Union army of 94,000 commanded by General George Meade would collide with a Confederate force of

72,000 commanded by Robert E. Lee. Residents hid in their cellars as artillery shells and bullets whistled overhead and through their homes. Although most of the fighting occurred in the surrounding countryside, the town saw its own share of the fighting, with the blood of wounded and dead pooling in the streets. The courthouse, train station, churches, and homes were filled with the wounded and dying. Piles of amputated arms and legs accumulated outside of buildings expropriated to become makeshift hospitals. In the aftermath, the stench of rotting corpses of men and animals alike, as well as the tons of excrement from the tens of thousands remaining alive, was so intense that residents put peppermint oil on their nostrils and kept their windows closed for weeks.

With the male population of the United States decimated, and hardly a family escaping the touch of death and destruction, whether directly or indirectly, the generation of survivors who lived through the American Civil War would be scarred like few before or after them. It would be nearly fifty more years before the United States was drawn into another great conflict, this time of world proportion, the carnage of which would fall primarily on the continent of Europe.

WWI, from a technological standpoint, was in many ways an extension, or second chapter, of the human butchery that took place during the American Civil War, but this time it would be the European population who would most suffer the slaughter and devastation. Onto the European countryside came trench warfare tactics on a scale that dwarfed anything like that practiced in the earlier American conflict. It also brought from earlier wars cavalry and infantry bayonet charges, only to find they were no match for mechanized warfare, which included the first armored vehicles that later came to be known as tanks or, to the Germans, as Panzers. The machine-gun, now much evolved and improved over its Civil War predecessor, kept watch over great expanses of barbed-wire terrain, known as the "no mans' land" that separated the opposing belligerents. War and death now came from the sky with the recent invention of the airplane, as well as from beneath the sea with the first large-scale deployment of U-boats or submarines by Germany. And probably most feared was the grizzly death brought by clouds of lethal gas that caused approximately 1.3 million casualties, about 90,000 of which were fatal.

While less than 10% effective from a lethality standpoint, gas or chemical warfare in WWI was a formidable weapon for the fear it instilled and the effects it had on morale amongst the troops. The two forms most used in this conflict were chlorine and mustard gas. Chlorine gas caused extreme eye irritation, which would immediately inhibit battle performance and, if inhaled, would mix with fluids in the lungs to form hydrochloric acid. The immediate symptoms were coughing and vomiting, and if, as in most cases, it did not cause death, it would probably cause permanent lung damage and associated disabilities. Mustard gas was the most commonly used, and its immediate effect was as a skin irritant, which caused chemical burns on the skin with blisters that oozed yellow fluid. If inhaled, it had similar internal effects to the respiratory system. Such was the horror of these weapons that they were subsequently banned by the Geneva Protocol of 1925.

For little more than four years, from 1914 into 1918, all the major world powers, and many lesser powers, would come to be engaged in this predominantly European conflict. Combined, these warring powers would place on the battlefield of this conflict some 70 million combatants, nearly half of which, or 31 million, would become casualties of the war, and of those nearly 10 million were fatal. The civilian populations of the warring

Europeans did not fare much better with a death toll of approximately eight million, approximately six million of which came from famine and disease. Of the civilian dead, the vast majority came from just three countries:

- ❖ Serbia, with a total population of approximately 4.5 million, lost 450,000 to 800,000 to malnutrition and disease, representing 10% to 18% of their total population.

- ❖ The Ottoman Empire, with a total population of approximately 21.5 million, lost an estimated 1 million to malnutrition and disease and another 1.5 million to military action or crimes against humanity, representing 12% of their total population.

- ❖ Russia, with a total population of approximately, 175 million lost an estimated 750,000 to malnutrition and disease and another 400,000 to military action or crimes against humanity, representing 0.66% of their total population.

Although not engaged in the war, Iran's civilian population suffered more severely than any of the belligerents. As an indirect consequence of the war, malnutrition and disease took the lives of some eight to ten million of a population of 19 million, thereby wiping out approximately half of their total population. Another indirect consequence, or offshoot of the war, was the Russian Revolution, which started in 1917 and claimed another seven to twelve million casualties. All tolled, WWI was responsible for some 40 million casualties, excluding tangential consequences, such as those in Iran and Russia. For the next two decades that followed, this conflict was commonly referred to as the "Great War" and/or "The War to End All Wars," not becoming known as the First World War until the end of the 1930s when a second hellacious world conflict of even greater proportions began. The Second World War would go on to eventually eclipse the death and destruction of its predecessor by a considerable margin.

WWII has particular significance for a multitude of reasons. For this writer, and the context of this narrative, it was not just a world conflict, which had taken the greatest toll of life in human history, but its place in time is near enough to the present that it is still at least on the margin of the public's general consciousness. In fact, at the time of this writing it is estimated that nearly 500,000 U.S. veterans of that conflict are still alive today, although this number is diminishing at a rate of more than 350 per day. Although a fairly recent historical occurrence, casualty figures are still varied. The most generally accepted, but at the same time most likely conservative, estimated death toll for WWII is approximately 60 million, with about 20 million coming from military deaths, and about 40 million from civilian deaths.

WWII similar to WWI was a continuation of the technological advances in warfare that proved so effective in the mass bloodletting and destruction of the American Civil War and WWI. WWII also advanced the mechanized warfare first implemented in WWI exponentially and on an industrialized scale. Armies and munitions could now be moved in large quantities by ship to most any corner of the globe. Death both from above with Flying Fortresses and from sea by the massive guns aboard naval ships could be delivered beyond enemy lines in mass. And the concept of total warfare, having been tested with brutal effectiveness by Sherman during the American Civil War in his march through the South to the sea, was now directed from the sky at not just military targets, but industrial targets and civilian populations alike. In WWII it began with the London Blitz — the German bombing of the English capital for 76 consecutive nights that killed an estimated 20,000 people. The primary refuge for many a Londoner during those long and fearful nights was the London Underground (the subway system). Although not resulting in total or even near-total destruction of London, the war left many other European cities at its end looking more like the surface of the moon than any semblance of advanced civilization. Some of the most notable for the severity of destruction and death toll are listed as follows:

<u>In Europe by conventional bombing and fire-bombing:</u>

❖ Kassel (February to March 1945) - 10,000 dead

❖ Darmstadt (September 1943 to February 1944) - 12,300 dead

❖ Pforzheim (April 1944 to March 1945) - 21,200 dead

❖ Berlin (1940 through 1945) - 20,000 to 50,000 dead

❖ Dresden (October 1944 to April 1945) - 25,000 dead

❖ Hamburg (September 1939 to April 1945) - 42,600 dead

BERLIN, GERMANY (POST-WWII) – Ruins of the Reichstag in Berlin after the city's capture by the Red Army in 1945.

DRESDEN, GERMANY (POST-WWII) – Remains of Dresden after a continued three day and night raid where the British RAF and American Army Air Forces dropped more than 3,900 tons of high explosive and incendiary bombs.

<u>In Japan by conventional bombing and fire-bombing:</u>

❖ Osaka (March to August 1945) - 10,000 dead

❖ Tokyo (November 1944 to August 1945) - 100,000 dead

In Japan by the Atomic Bombs:

❖ Hiroshima (August 6, 1945) - 90,000 to 150,000 dead

❖ Nagasaki (August 9, 1945) - 40,000 to 80,000 dead

TOKYO, JAPAN (POST-WWII) – Remains of Tokyo after repeated fire bombings by the United States Air and Naval Forces.

HIROSHIMA (POST-WWII) – Remains of Hiroshima after the first nuclear bomb was dropped on the city in 1945.

In part a result of the mass bombings during WWII, huge portions of the civilian populations of Europe and Asia were in disarray, with refugees fleeing the cities and advancing armies. Many civilians died from disease, starvation, massacres, and deliberate genocide. While an estimated six million Jews died at the hands of the Nazis in the Holocaust, it is estimated that another five to eleven million non-Jews were systematically killed as part of Nazi ideological policies. Under Stalin it is estimated that more than 3.5 million perished in Soviet Gulags (forced labor camps). In Asia and the South Pacific, it is estimated that three to ten million civilians died as part of the Japanese occupation of China in which some 50,000 to 300,000 Chinese were raped and murdered. All tolled, it is estimated that about 3% of the world's total population perished during this war.

Both WWI and WWII were global events with the vast majority of hostilities in WWI occurring on the European continent, and in the case of WWII the majority of hostilities taking place in Europe, the South Pacific, and in Asia. With the exception of the Japanese attack on Pearl Harbor in WWII that resulted in about 2,400 military deaths and 1,100 wounded, as well as about 100 civilians killed and wounded, the U.S. civilian population escaped the devastation experienced by their counterparts in the major theaters of these two wars. Even the casualties experienced by the U.S. military, while significant when viewed in isolation, did not approach that of some of the other combatants. In WWI the U.S. military suffered less than 500,000 casualties, of which about 117,000 were fatalities, more than half of which came from the 1918 influenza outbreak. In WWII the U.S. military suffered about 1.1 million casualties, of which a little more than 400,000 were fatalities.

The sum total of U.S. fatalities from all the armed conflicts the U.S. has been engaged in since WWII is slightly more than 100,000. The vast majority of which come from just two major wars. The following is a listing of those two conflicts along with the four largest of the other engagements to provide context for the range in size of these conflicts:

- ❖ The Korean War (1950-1953) — 36,500 U.S. fatalities
- ❖ The Vietnam War (1955-1975) — 58,2000 U.S. fatalities
- ❖ The Afghan War (2001-present) — 2,200 U.S. fatalities
- ❖ The Iraq War (2003-2011) — 4,500 U.S. fatalities
- ❖ The Gulf War (1990-1991) — 294 U.S. fatalities
- ❖ Beirut Deployment (1982-1984) — 266 U.S. fatalities

When measured against the U.S. population during the post-WWII era, as well as the mere fact that these numbers are measured in the tens of thousands, or hundreds, rather than in the millions from earlier periods, it would be difficult to argue that we have not been living in the greatest period of peace and tranquility than that of any other time in history, and surely exceeding that of the Pax Romana.

Chapter 4

Economics

"The trouble with Socialism is that eventually you run out of other people's money."

—*Margaret Thatcher*

At the end of the *Prologue* you may have noted, or maybe not, that mention was made of a coincidental near simultaneous concurrence of two historical events. It is the combination of these two events in the early 1800s that made possible the rapid and accelerated advances in humanity at the end of that century and through the 1900s to our present day. We are only on Chapter 4, but if you have not already gleaned it from the preceding chapters, I will summarize it here: Prior to the occurrence of these two events, advancements in humanity and/or the standard of living for all of mankind through the millennia were for all intents and purposes nearly immeasurable. Too often overlooked for the synergy of their combined prodigious importance, not just for the United States and the developed world, but for the world as a whole, the combination of these two events made possible the multitude of successive and exponentially increasing advancements that we so often and casually take for granted today. So, if you haven't already looked back to the *Prologue,* here they are:

1. The Enlightenment and in turn the Industrial Revolution.

2. The Founding of the United States, specifically its Democracy and Free Market Capitalist Economy.

The Enlightenment and subsequent Industrial Revolution may well have gotten us to where we are today on their own, but without capitalism to drive innovation and productivity through specialization, it would surely not have been until sometime in the very distant future. It was American freedom and the right of self-determination, along with property rights and the legal framework to support the ownership of the fruits of one's own labor, that released the engine of capitalism, thereby driving this advancement at such an accelerated rate. The two most important attributes of capitalism, which were inherent to this freedom and unique to the rest of the World at the time that the United States was founded were:

1. Property rights and the associated contract laws required to support the enforcement of those rights for the people.

2. Risk/reward proposition and associated moral hazard, which I will define as one's ownership of the results of their decisions and/or actions for success or failure.

In simple terms and taken together, the individual maintains ownership of the fruits of their labor, irrespective of how abundant they may be or even if the fruit turns out to be inedible. As simple and intuitive as the motivation this basic principle instills in individuals and collectively as nations, it is just as easily overlooked and even occasionally demonized. The primal and innate drive for one to work and act in their own best interest is what drives innovation and the engine of capitalism. Probably not so coincidentally, it was first notably observed, or more accurately written about, in Adam Smith's work entitled *The Wealth of Nations,* first published in 1776. Adam Smith noted that the collective result of the masses of individuals acting and making decisions in their own best interests effectively and efficiently moves capital goods, supplying them to meet demand. He referred to this free and naturally occurring exchange as the invisible hand. Smith concisely portrayed this phenomenon by stating, "It is not from the benevolence of the butcher, the brewer, or the baker, that we expect our dinner, but from their regard to their own interest."

Following the American Revolution, and a brief period of government under the Articles of Confederation, the United States Constitution, that we know today, was ratified in 1789, not in small measure by the efforts of Alexander Hamilton, James Madison, and John Jay through their writings simply titled *The Federalist*. Subsequently, on April 30, 1789, George Washington took his oath of office as the first President of the United States. One of Washington's great attributes, among a multitude of great attributes, was to surround himself with the best and the brightest, and in his first administration this characteristic did not fail him when he appointed Alexander Hamilton as the Nation's first Secretary of the Treasury. It was Hamilton who laid the groundwork and foundation for the Capitalistic economy we have today. Of his more prominent contemporaries from the founding generation, Hamilton was becoming somewhat lost to the public consciousness in recent decades, and in fact consideration was even being given to replacing his portrait on the ten-dollar bill. Fortunately, however, his identity and accomplishments have found a new resurgence in recent years due to Lin-Manuel Miranda's hit Broadway play appropriately titled *Hamilton*. If you've had the opportunity to see the play or better yet to have read the biography by Ron Chernow, which was the inspiration for Miranda's musical, you will be aware of the extremely humble and bleak beginnings that Hamilton rose from. His story is an early example of the opportunity found nowhere else but in the United States of America.

In brief, Hamilton was born out of wedlock on the Caribbean island of Nevis in 1757, although there is conflicting evidence that it may have actually been 1755. His mother died of yellow fever in 1768, leaving him orphaned at the age of either 11 or 13, depending upon his correct year of birth. His intellectual aptitude at an early age caught the favor of prominent merchants and community leaders, compelling them to finance his travel to the English colonies in America to receive a formal education. His education at King's College (today's Columbia University) in New York City was interrupted by the Revolutionary War, and as an artillery officer during the defense of that city and in other subsequent engagements early in the war, his valor and intellectual aptitude were noted by several senior officers, eventually gaining the attention of General George Washington himself. He became George Washington's aide de camp, serving by his side and executing a wide variety of high-level duties with decorum and command well beyond his years. There are those who view Washington's relationship with Hamilton to be that of a surrogate father figure, and although their relationship may well have evolved as such, the fact was that Washington found Hamilton's abilities and service as his top aide indispensable. Such was their relationship that Washington resisted Hamilton's persistent desire for a field command and the opportunity for military glory. Washington finally relented near the end of the war, giving him command of three battalions at the Battle of Yorktown, where he indeed gained the combat glory and notoriety he fiercely sought and deserved. Most importantly it was during and after the war that Hamilton solidified Washington's confidence in his intellectual virtues, specifically in economic and financial matters, appointing him to be the nation's first Secretary of the Treasury. Over the course of little more than four years serving as Treasury Secretary, Hamilton's list of accomplishments is unequaled. Some of the more notable include:

- ❖ Reorganization of an oppressively burdensome war debt and establishing a revenue system of customs duties and excise taxes to attack and harness that debt.

- ❖ Creation of a national bank (The First Bank of the United States) to increase public and private credit.

- ❖ Creation of the U.S. Mint to establish and put into circulation a common national currency.

- ❖ Founding of the Revenue Cutter Service to patrol coastal waters and fight smuggling, thereby insuring the collection of tariffs.

Fundamental to his formation of the foregoing, he maintained that liberty and property rights were inseparable and that contracts, both public and private, need to be honored affirming the concept of moral hazard. His efforts secured the confidence and respect of other nations, thereby establishing the solvency and creditworthiness of the United States and, in time, serving to form the basis of the economic prosperity that followed and is with us today.

In Washington, DC, great memorials have been erected to Washington and Jefferson, as well as many other great American founders and leaders. By comparison there is a modest bronze statue of Alexander

STATUE OF ALEXANDER HAMILTON (WASH-INGTON DC) – This statue commemorates the first Secretary of the Treasury. It stands on the south side of the U.S. Treasury Building, adjacent to the White House.

Hamilton, which stands in his memory on the south side of the U.S. Treasury building. However, for a memorial more fitting in stature and representative of the contributions this man made in laying the ground-work for the vibrant U.S. economy that survives to this day, one only needs to look at New York City itself, the world's financial capital and Hamilton's adopted home, where he was laid to rest in the heart of that city's financial district; his remains lie in the yard of Trinity Church, at the intersection of Wall Street and Broadway.

Up to the time of Adam Smith's scholarly economic work and the efforts of Hamilton in the early days of the United States, mercantilism was displacing feudalism as the most common form of economics practiced by the monarchial powers of Europe. Feudalism, which took various forms in Medieval Europe, generally refers to the relationship between lords (the land-holding class) and the peasants, known as vassals (who unlike serfs were free peoples). The peasants, who by paying homage to their lord, were granted tracts of land that the Lord retained the property rights or ownership of and were promised protection in exchange for military service and/or regular payments of produce or money. Mercan-tilism places the focus of economic policy on the nation's economy at the expense of rival national powers by aiming at accumulating mon-etary reserves through a positive balance of trade, generally achieved through high tariffs, which specifically target manufactured goods. It is still practiced to various degrees today, most notably by Germany, where it has been a primary factor in the economic success they have realized in recent decades over their European and other western peers.

In the years that followed, there were only a handful of economic ar-rangements tested and practiced to any significant degree around the world. We will address the four most prominent and notable, but first, we must acknowledge that variations in definition exist for all with the distinction between some easily and often blurred. With that said, the exception is capitalism, for which very clear distinctions can be drawn in comparison to the other three (communism, socialism, and fascism), with very little, if any, opportunity for confusion or overlap. First and foremost, capitalism is an economic system alone, whereas the other three are both interdependent economic and political constructs, much as the present-day theocracies of the Middle East are an inseparable intertwining of government and religion. In the case of the United States, capitalism as an economic system is paired with a political system in the form of a federal representative democracy.

In recent years there has been some resurgence in support of socialism in the United States, being touted as *democratic socialism*. Based upon the foregoing paragraph, one should surmise that this terminology is a concoction of an economic system with an incompatible political system. It is my belief that this is little more than a marketing strategy, an attempt to take an old and failed ideology and rebrand it. Yes, as they say, somewhat akin to putting lipstick on a pig. I could go on ad nauseam in support of what I and many others view as a hoax or a fraud on its followers, but instead, I will conveniently defer to Milton Friedman, who in his work *Capitalism and Freedom* wrote:

"It is widely believed that politics and economics are separate and largely unconnected; that individual freedom is a political problem and material welfare an economic problem; and that any kind of political arrangements can be combined with any kind of economic arrangements. The chief contemporary manifestation of this idea is the advocacy of *democratic socialism* by many who condemn out of hand the restrictions on individual freedom imposed by *totalitarian socialism* in Russia and who are persuaded that it is possible for a country to adopt the essential features of Russian economic arrangements and yet to ensure individual freedom through political arrangements. Such a view is a delusion, there is an intimate connection between economics and politics, that only certain combinations of political and economic arrangements are possible, and that in particular, a society which is socialist cannot also be democratic, in the sense of guaranteeing individual freedom."

Based upon his status as an economic scholar alone, the foregoing statement could easily stand on its own, but Friedman does go on in the same book to convincingly and quite definitively support this claim. It is also important to note here that when Friedman wrote these words, his references to Russia were directed at what is now the former Soviet Union.

Having dispelled the delusion of democratic socialism, we can now go on to look at the definitions of the earlier referenced four economic arrangements from an economic perspective (the political aspects of communism, socialism, and fascism are discussed in Chapter 6). Unlike capitalism, which is readily and generally consistently defined, the definitions of communism, socialism, and fascism tend to vary by source, sometimes overlapping and conflated with political nuance; therefore, the following definitions are an attempt to summarize the underlying common and generally accepted economic principles:

❖ Capitalism — This is a system of private individual or corporate ownership of capital goods; investments are determined by private decision and by prices, production, and the distribution of goods, which are determined mainly by competition in a free market (emphasis on the word "free").

❖ Communism — This is a system in which all property is owned in common or by the State and is made available by the State to all as needed; this is a theory advocating the elimination of private property.

❖ Socialism — This is a system in which private ownership of goods by individuals is retained, but the means of production, distribution, and exchange of goods are owned or strictly regulated by the State; this can be used as a transitional phase in supplanting capitalism with communism.

❖ Fascism — This is a system of private individual or corporate ownership of capital goods; however, private investment, production, and distribution of goods is strongly aligned, intertwined with, or controlled by a nationalistic agenda.

Neither communism nor fascism have much, if any, following in the United States, except for some very small and inconsequential segments of the population: Communism, primarily for economic reasons, because of its diametrically opposed position on the American foundational precept of private property, and fascism, primarily for social reasons, because of its autocratic nature and its social/racial uniformity that are so invariably in opposition with the acceptable norms of American society. However, socialism is seeing a resurgence, in no small measure, and it is becoming so pervasive that it can no longer be discounted. Its growing following is predominantly among younger segments of the population that have here-to-for been discounted due to the perception that their naïve innocence facilitates an emotional susceptibility to the promotion of a seemingly utopian proposition. Support has also been nurtured in broader segments of the population who view many of the social programs already in place (i.e. Social Security, Medicare, Medicaid, etc.) with sweeping favorability. And why not? Who can or would be willing to argue against the equality of social welfare for all? Again, I will defer to Milton Friedman who succinctly stated:

> *"A society that puts equality before freedom will get neither. A society that puts freedom before equality will get a high degree of both."*

Even if we don't look at socialism as a transitional phase toward the type of communism practiced in the former U.S.S.R. (which collapsed in 1991) and believe that forms of socialism can be sustained in a measured form without totalitarianism, force, and/or coercion, how will we know when we near the precipice of the tipping point of no return? It is true that most transitions to extreme forms of socialism or communism, such as in the former Soviet Union or those still in force in Cuba, came into being through abrupt and violent insurrections. There is, however, one fairly recent case where transitional socialism crept into a comparatively prosperous capitalistic economy and passed through the point of no return to a totalitarian state. Although current promoters of socialism shy away from using Venezuela as an example of what they espouse, it was once proclaimed the "Socialism of the 21st Century" by the former President of Venezuela, Hugo Chavez, and many other supporters (at the height of Venezuela's oil revenues). It is indeed a perfect example of a complete transition from capitalism to socialism then to a failed state and is a cautionary tale for anyone committed to the promise of socialism. The following provides a timeline of some of the major events in this specific example, but to be fair, it must be noted that Venezuela's comparative prosperity over other Latin American countries has always been tied to, and is somewhat a function of, its vast oil reserves, and its economic conditions consistently fluctuated significantly with the rise and fall of world oil prices.

1973 — Venezuela nationalizes its oil and steel industries.

1998 — Hugo Chavez is elected President and institutes a new constitution, socialist and populist economic policies, and social policies funded by high oil prices.

2001 — President Chavez utilizes an Enabling Act to pass laws aimed at redistributing land and wealth.

2005 — President Chavez signs a decree on land reform to eliminate Venezuela's large estates and benefit the rural poor.

2007 — In January, President Chavez announces that key energy and telecom companies will be nationalized under the Enabling Act. In June, two leading U.S. oil companies, Exxon Mobile and Conoco Philips, have their Orinoco Belt operations expropriated by the Venezuelan government.

2009 — Voters approve a referendum to abolish term limits, thereby, allowing Hugo Chavez to run for President again in 2012.

2010 — President Chavez devalues the Bolivar (Venezuelan Currency) to boost oil revenue after the economy shrinks 5.8% in the last quarter of 2009.

2012 — Venezuelan National Assembly enacts the Control of Arms, Munitions and Disarmament Law with the explicit aim to "disarm all citizens," and the government extends price controls on basic goods to fight inflation. President Chavez threatens to expropriate companies that do not comply with price controls.

2013 President Hugo Chavez dies at the age of 58 and is replaced by his chosen successor, Nicolas Maduro.

2014 — The government announces cuts to public spending as oil prices reach a four-year low.

2016 — Hundreds of thousands of people take part in a protest in Caracas, calling for the removal of President Maduro and accusing him of being responsible for the economic crisis.

2018 — The UN announces that two million people had fled Venezuela to neighboring countries since 2014. The inflation rate in Venezuela hits 1,000,000%.

Besides socialism's tendency to transition a state to totalitarianism and the usurping of individual rights and freedoms through force and coercion (the most common and seemingly least intrusive form being taxation), it is a killer of initiative and innovation. What's the last major innovation that you've seen come from a socialistic country? In fact, you may find it difficult to identify any innovation of any significance at all coming from a socialistic country, even those lesser extreme forms in Western Europe held up by supporters as successful models of socialism currently in practice. And from what country and form of economics has the lion's share of all innovation come from in the past 100 to 200 years? No need to answer, it was a rhetorical question. But sorry, I cannot help myself; of course, it is the United States of America. Even with the deluge of regulation and taxation placed upon the U.S. economy in the last 100 years, America remains the country with the most dynamic economic system in the world.

Those still in denial will point to some perceived flaws in capitalism; the most commonly cited is "income and/or wealth inequality," and to counter, we have already provided Milton Friedman's response above. However, so prominent is this topic in politics, and the media today, it is explored in detail in Chapter 6. Two other prominent runners-up are: first, the decline of the U.S. industrial economy from its height in the 1950s and 1960s; and second, extreme economic swings, specifically with respect to extreme lows, such as the Great Recession and the Great Depression, as well as the Irrational Exuberance of the late 1990s and the mid 2000s driven by the dot-com and housing bubbles. The criticism of capitalism for these events is misguided and dispelled as follows.

With respect to the U.S. economic slide from the post-WWII boom:

The two decades that followed WWII created somewhat of an economic illusion of what was possible or could be expected in our, or any, free market economy. With the single exception of the United States, the manufacturing capacities and infrastructure of the world's other great industrial powers were all but destroyed by the war, thereby making the United States a near monopoly in the supply of manufactured goods for all world commerce. As those economies and their industrial bases began to reemerge from the war's devastation (with considerable assistance from the U.S.), demand for U.S. goods declined globally, and market forces reallocated resources accordingly around the world as a whole. It is true that imbalances have emerged and exist today to the detriment of the United States economy, with the pendulum having now swung significantly to the opposite extreme, but this is predominately the result mercantile practices by competing nations (most notably China) and is not a symptom of free trade capitalistic forces.

China's considerable economic rise and expansion in recent years, interestingly enough, has been touted as evidence of success by proponents of both capitalism and socialism, but for very different reasons. This success is attributed to China's adoption of marginal capitalist practices by capitalists and at the same time attributed to China's socialistic policies by those in support of socialism. While there may be some validity to both schools of thought, and this author has obvious leanings toward crediting the adoption of some capitalistic practices, the credit by and large should go to that country's coordinated and all-out assault on the exploitation of other global capitalistic economies — specifically, the pirating of copyrighted and patented products of competitors, theft and/or forced transfer of intellectual property, currency and pricing manipulation, etc. The simplest and clearest example of this reality is the fact that from their sudden economic ascent in world trade, there have been few notable innovations other than the ability to reproduce products developed by others at significantly lower costs. And here I'm deliberately being factitious, since this is more a function of the availability of low-cost labor, which few would consider innovative.

With respect to economic extremes of so-called boom and bust periods:

Most all economies, but indeed accentuated in free market economies, have a pervasive force of market psychology, or more specifically confidence, and the extremes of a herd mentality. This force has the ability to take economic events, good or bad, and extenuate them sometimes to extremes well beyond any rational explanation, but this cause and effect is less about economics than it is about human nature itself. While it may only be natural for one to harbor underlying concerns that this aspect of economics has the ability to make capitalism appear to be very fragile at times, as evidenced by the many panics that have occurred throughout history, it has almost at the same time proven it to be very resilient by the subsequent recoveries that have always followed. It is not my intent to attempt to oversimplify what can be very complex subject matter, and indeed, the underlying causes of economic cycles are very much debated amongst economic scholars, of which I do not pretend to be one. The point here is that the extremes that these cycles are sometimes driven to are based upon little more than fear, which is a considerable force in nature.

Historically, most people are cognizant of the Great Depression and in most of our lifetimes the Great Recession. The fact is that before and after both of these events there have been many other lesser known cycles that have occurred with successive regularity, many of which were quite extreme in their time. Today, this historical track record is now lost to the cognizance of much of the general public. One of the most extreme and bizarre of all time took place well before the capitalistic economy of the United States was ever any figment of anyone's imagination. Approximately 150 years before the American Revolution in the Dutch Republic (modern day Holland), speculation on tulip bulbs began to take on inconceivably absurd proportions. At its height bulbs were selling for as much as 3,000 to 4,000 guilders. This was at a time when the average skilled craftsman earned 300 guilders a year. That means that flower bulbs, having an intrinsic value of little more than the potential beauty of some future flower, were valued at more than ten times that of an average workers annual income. In a three-month period in early 1637, the speculative bubble burst, destroying the artificially inflated wealth of many a so-called investor.

As bleak as perceived circumstances may seemed to have been by or for many who experienced the Great Depression or Great Recession, the take away here is that even at its depth, conditions for even some of those most impacted were far better than that during prior periods, especially when compared to that of those under other economic forms. Had you lived in the Ukraine in 1932 or 1933, you may have been among the millions who died of starvation due to central planning decisions made by the Soviet Union under Joseph Stalin. Or, in more recent times, you could have been, and still yet today may be, enjoying the consistency and near monolithic uniformity of poverty in a country like Cuba. This poverty is a condition that has existed under totalitarian Cuba's socialism for more than a half century now.

So then, if the American economic system provides the greatest opportunity for prosperity that the world has ever known, what is the real problem with our economy and the current generation's perception of it? I believe the former Federal Reserve Chairman, Alan Greenspan, had put his finger squarely upon it when he stated:

> *"The number one problem in today's generation and economy is the lack of financial literacy."*

Unfortunately, in recent years the term capitalism has started to take on a connotation somewhat akin to that of a dirty word. Those seeking a strawman to blame for many a social woe target capitalism as the cause and in turn, with no substantive evidence, have elevated socialism as the cure. With no historical validation and considerable evidence to the contrary, socialism has seemingly been gaining favoritism, if for no other reason than it may simply sound better or have a better ring to it than capitalism appears to. With logic derived from a grounded historical and economic understanding being figuratively thrown to the wind, proponents of capitalism may need to resort to re-branding, which is a strategy that has been successfully practiced and has served politicians and those in marketing well for years. Such is the case of socialism being re-branded as democratic socialism. With education in history and economics severely lacking, the solution to the conundrum observed by Alan Greenspan could be as simple as merely calling capitalism what it is: the free enterprise system.

NYC THE SEAT OF AMERICAN CAPITALISM – This city manifests the product of Alexander Hamilton's efforts as the first Secretary of the Treasury. He rests in the financial district amidst the base of the NYC skyline.

"American exceptionalism" is another phrase that has come to be frowned upon in recent years. Unfortunately, its detractors have come to label and view it as a proclamation of egocentric elitism. It is rather a reasonably accurate description of the unique and unparalleled social and economic prosperity of the United States in little over 200 years as evidenced in the foregoing chapters. Obviously, an abstract phrase, such as American exceptionalism, means different things to different people, and the number of different definitions you could get is more than likely only dependent upon the number of people you ask. Apart from any specific answers obtained in an attempt to define it, they will all fall into two general schools of thought: those who define it in a positive light, and those who do not. And for those who do not, they are generally looking at it from a perception of it being an elitist phrase based in conceit. However, falling back to Alan Greenspan's observation, cited above, and acknowledging that an ignorance of history and economics is not just plausible, but likely pervasive, one may well draw a different conclusion. Hopefully, this chapter provided an adequate historical context, along with a necessary complement in economics, which will allow us to converge on a consistent conclusion: That the United States, through the wisdom, hard work, and sacrifice of its founding fathers, established a unique republic based upon democratic principles, and coupling this form of government with a free market capitalistic economy formed the foundation for the prosperity that the American people have come to enjoy and in no small measure have shared with the rest of the world.

Chapter 5

The Environment

"Sheep, like people, are ungovernable when hungry."

—*John Muir*

In recent years there have been comparisons of certain environmental rhetoric, coming from more far-left zealots, to that of religious dogma. More and more, the fervor being played out, through the questioning and often fervent challenging of personal beliefs and in turn the pledging of one's faith in such beliefs, does give credence to and substantiates such an analogy. After all, is not religion synonymous with faith? On no other topic is this the case more than that of "global warming" or "climate change" (the name of the religion had to be changed when some of the earlier prophecies failed to come to fruition). The build-up to the fatalistic doctrine that exists today for the parishioners devoted to this faith got its foothold in 2006 with Al Gore's film *An Inconvenient Truth.* Due to the awards and renown it garnered, there is a high probability that even if you have not seen the film, you may well at least have some awareness of it and its subject matter. The existential nature of this apocalyptic prophecy was bolstered by the extreme and record hurricane season of the prior year, which included the devastation of Hurricane Katrina. Since I am now dwelling in religious semantics, I have a confession to make. Shortly after the film came out, I did see it, and having seen it, I do confess that I believe it does make a compelling argument for the probability that man, through the use of fossil fuels, could well have an impact on the world's climate. But then making a compelling argument is one thing; whereas, claiming that the science supporting it is conclusive and definitive is quite another. Such blind devotion to any cause should serve to increase suspicion, particularly in those who may already be suspicious of such proclamations. Most disconcerting about this congregation's belief system is the fear mongering and threats of doom that have proliferated.

The real truth lies in the fact that science is not certain; it's rarely incontrovertible, or indisputable, and it is very much subject to change. Take for example the *Newsweek* article of April 28, 1975, by Peter Gwynne, titled *The Cooling World*, and many other similar articles appearing during the 1970s in publications, such as *Popular Science, Science Digest, The New York Times* and *Los Angeles Times, The Christian Science Monitor,* and *National Geographic*, etc. These articles forecasted a coming ice age. So, was it "fake news" then or now? Bad science then or now? Devout climate change true believers counter with reasonable arguments, such as the science and climatic modeling has gotten much better since the 1970s. But then this argument makes my point exactly; science is always changing. And what will the science be, say, 40 years from now? Well, we just don't know, but if we believe the politicians and their disciples running around with their hair on fire, proclaiming that if the effects of climate change are not reversed in twelve years we're all going to die, it hardly matters, now does it?

Fatalistic profits and their cults have come to us periodically and regularly over the course of history with varying notoriety; some garnering amazingly significant followings. Let us take a look at three of the most prominent in the history of the United States:

❖ William Miller (The Millerites) — In the 1830s William Miller, a Baptist preacher from upstate New York, shared his beliefs with respect to the second coming of Christ. Based upon his interpretation of the scriptures, he believed that Christ's return would usher in the apocalypse somewhere between 1843 and 1844, ultimately arriving at a specific date of October 22, 1844. At the height of his following, there were estimated to have been as many as one million believers. As the prophesied date approached, there were reports of Millerites selling or giving away all of their worldly possessions; some even donning white robes for their ascension. When the 22nd came and went, there were successive recalculations of the forecasted end, but the prophecy remains unfulfilled to this day.

❖ Marshall Applewhite (Heaven's Gate) — Marshall Applewhite and his partner, Bonnie Nettles, believing they were divine messengers, began traveling the U.S. to spread their beliefs in 1973. By the late 1970s, Applewhite began to gain a group of committed followers. Known as Heaven's Gate, they shared a belief that they would be visited by extraterrestrials, who would aid them in ascending to their spaceship. In 1996 they learned of the approach to Earth of the comet Hale-Bopp and believed that it was trailed by the spaceship that was to be their rendezvous with destiny. In March of 1997, the group of thirty-nine devoted followers, including Applewhite, wearing their Heaven's Gate insignia and Nike shoes, committed suicide by taking barbiturates with alcohol and placing bags over their heads.

❖ Rev. Jim Jones (Peoples Temple) — In the 1950s the Rev. Jim Jones started the Peoples Temple in Indiana, later moving along with much of his congregation to California in 1965. In 1977, he moved, along with about 1,000 of his followers, to a commune he had established in Guyana, South America, naming it Jonestown. It was during his time in Guyana when he began to propagate a belief in what he termed "translation," wherein he and his followers would die together and go to a higher place to live in bliss. Amid allegations of human rights abuse, Congressman Leo Ryan led a group of reporters and relatives of Temple members on a fact-finding mission to Jonestown in November of 1978. After the visit Jones had the Congressmen and four others killed before they could depart. Later that same day, Jones led his followers in a mass suicide. Many drank willingly from vats of cyanide-laced Kool-Aid, thus giving us the phrase "Kool-Aid drinker" or to "drink the Kool-Aid," which today is synonymous with blind faith.

In a way, similar to climate science and/or climatic modeling, but far more accurate, was Newtonian physics. From the time that Sir Isaac Newton developed his three laws of physics, they produced accurate predictions that were consistently verified over time, making them seemingly incontrovertible and indisputable. Then, some 200 years later, along came a wild-haired guy from Germany by the name of Albert Einstein. He showed mathematically and later proved experimentally that the properties of mass and time would vary when approaching the speed of light, at which point Newton's laws came apart. Without the work of Einstein, many of the technological advances we have become accustomed to would not exist today. In fact, without the continual evolution of science, we would still be living in the 1700s. Much more commonly observed by everyday people are the almost annual contradictory publications of scientific research and studies on the health benefits of coffee and/or red wine. For example, there will be articles about the health benefits of coffee and similarly for red wine, then there will be new articles refuting the benefits of these and even articles citing possible health risks. Regular contradictions on both go as far back as my memory allows me to recall. Therefore, when someone tells you that the science is settled on anything, you should naturally be suspect to whatever argument they are making.

On the hysteria and alarming prophecies of doom and death if action is not taken to resolve this "existential threat" within twelve years, if not hyperbole, then the same prophets should be honest enough to state that we're all nearly as good as dead already. Are we to actually believe that our vote for any one of these prophets, or even if all the politicians promoting this prophecy were to be elected to office, that the United States legislature could accomplish something tangible to affect the alleged threat? Particularly, could it be done within the time frame they state is necessary to mitigate this prophecy of doom? These are the same people who cannot even balance a budget, and of whom the most notable and/ or significant of accomplishments include the ability to name a post office. Irrespective of the government's inability to solve problems, real or perceived, their targets are also often misdirected or misguided. Of the top three producers of CO_2 emissions, the United States ranks number two, with emissions dropping by more than 10% since 2005. The number one producer is China, with emissions about double that of the United States and increasing by about 50% since 2005. Number three is India, with emissions about half that of the United States but increasing by nearly 90% since 2005. Why focus on just these three? Well, they account for approximately half of all the world emissions, and if nothing is done about the current rates of increase by China and India, any further measures taken by the United States would be inconsequential. If climate change is the real existential global threat of our lifetime as proclaimed, then the real enemies to mankind are China and India. The only logical course of action would, therefore, be to declare war on them unless they change their ways. After all was there not a politician who recently proclaimed that this was the greatest threat facing us since the Second World War and required a similar mobilization and response? But if we take this line of reasoning further, isn't the underlying problem overpopulation, in which case an all-out sneak nuclear attack would be the most logical approach? Obviously, neither approach is offered as a viable or serious suggestion, but instead, they are intended to provide perspective to the folly of an issue already blown well beyond any rational proportion.

The Green New Deal recently proposed by an exalted "Messiah" of this doomsday prophecy has already been given far more deliberation than it deserves, even having been voted upon in the Senate. For weeks it received much promotion and debate by politicians and the press alike — by both those pledging their faith and support, as well as others discrediting it based upon attempts to estimate its fiscal absurdity. Still many other politicians not even on the national level, such as mayors and governors, mostly in New York, California and Illinois, pledged their efforts in the fight. In the end, of the 100 Senators, the Green New Deal received 57 "no" votes and the other 43 members are on the record as voting "present." So how did all the support dissolve, seemingly overnight? Well, because deep down, the vast majority of political proponents realize a truth that they can't admit publicly or discuss at cocktail parties with their peers for fear of being ostracized. That it was and is a fraud, simply used to harvest emotional support for the power of its promoters. Another consideration, apart from any emotional or counter fiscal arguments, is to simply question whether it is even remotely possible that any substantive segment of mankind would ever seriously give consideration to going back to a pre-industrialized standard of living? And far from debating the validity of this prophecy, can anyone really believe that government could be the solution? If the prophecy of doom is real, our only real hope is that capitalism will be the vehicle that drives the development of cost-effective alternatives to the energy we have all become so dependent upon. Finally, if meteorologists can forecast weather five days out with only a 90% accuracy, and that accuracy drops to less than 50% when forecasting beyond seven days, how accurate should anyone expect a climatologist to be when projecting decades into the future? Furthermore, modern-day meteorological forecasting has the advantage of huge amounts of very accurate real time data as a resource; whereas, climatologists are dependent upon a much more limited data set, which is generally derived through empirical inference.

Aside from the hyperbole about climate projections that sucks all the oxygen out of the room, what is the real overall condition of our environment, and how does it compare to historical conditions? Well, the short answer is that for most of the developed world it is quite good when compared to historical standards. But note that I did use the caveat the "developed world." Much of the undeveloped world and many countries presently in what may be referred to as being in a developing industrialization phase (i.e. India, China, and much of Southeast Asia) are comparable to, or considerably worse, than during the industrialization period of the United States and Europe in the late 1800s and early 1900s. In recent years, of the world's rivers consistently ranking as the most polluted, at least seven of the top ten are found in India, China, and Southeast Asia and include such names as the Ganges River in India, The Citarum River in Indonesia, and The Yellow River in China. To drink from any of these rivers is to literally take your life into your own hands.

Each year hundreds of thousands, if not millions, are estimated to die from water-borne diseases attributed to these water sources, and yet millions more are dependent upon these same rivers for their sustenance. It should additionally be noted that these rivers alone are estimated to be the source of nearly 90% of the plastics deposited in the world's oceans.

THE CITARUM RIVER, INDONESIA – Reputed to be the most polluted river in the world.

For the developed world, only two rivers are generally ranked among the top ten most polluted, and they include the Mississippi River in the United States and the Sarno River in Italy. Similarly, air quality in North America and Europe is generally quite good compared to prior industrialized periods; whereas, in other parts of the world it has deteriorated at a similar rate as that of the water quality in the same geographical areas. Historically water and air quality in North America and Europe has seen periods of severe negative environmental impact, and so, too, the preindustrial deforestation of Europe had negative environmental impacts. Over the course of the millennia prior to the industrial revolution, many of Europe's forests were cleared for farming and grazing and harvested for the construction of shelter and for fuel to heat these shelters in winter. One of the great natural resources recognized and exploited in the New World, and a principle draw of settlers to North America, were its nearly pristine virgin forests. Ironically, it is fossil fuels (i.e. coal, oil, and natural gas) used as fuels for heating in lieu of wood that ultimately helped to mitigate the continued deforestation in Europe and much of North America, but today they are now demonized for their CO_2 emissions. Another natural resource that was early to be identified and exploited was the abundance of fish in the Hudson, the Chesapeake, and off the coast of North America. In the rivers of Europe at the time scarcely a fish could be found, as the Seine in Paris, the Thames in London, the Rhine in Berlin, and the Tiber in Rome were all open sewers for hundreds of years and continued to be up until the advent of sanitary sewer systems and waste treatment in the early 1900s. With the settlement of North America and its subsequent urbanization, it was not long before this great wilderness and the fisheries of the eastern seaboard began to resemble those of their European forefathers. With the advent of the Industrial Age, the environments of both Europe and North America began to deteriorate at an accelerated rate up to the 1960s, during which time the issue reached a pivotal point where it could no longer be ignored.

During the "environmental crisis" of the 1960s, extreme environmental catastrophes were becoming more and more commonplace events in the news consumed by Americans. It was not uncommon to read regular reports and to see news reports on television of occurrences, including but not limited to regular and extreme smog events in New York City and Los Angeles, massive oil spills, and rivers catching fire. By 1966 major smog events were occurring regularly in New York City, hitting a milestone event during the Thanksgiving Holiday of that year. In a message to Congress, President Johnson, referring to the event, described it by stating that "a mass of heavily polluted air — filled with poisons from incinerators, industrial furnaces, power plants, car, bus, and truck engines — settled down upon the 16 million people of Greater New York." This event, in which the peak effects lasted about three days, is attributed with 168 fatalities. At least two other prior events of similar magnitude and consequence had occurred in New York City in 1953 and 1963. Although Los Angeles has had a notorious history with smog, surprisingly the worst recorded smog event was not in Los Angeles but in London, where in December of 1952 a great dense smog paralyzed the city for five days. So thick was the smog and so poor the visibility that it brought boat and shipping traffic on the River Thames to a halt, grounded air travel, and even cancelled trains. Automobile travel was so treacherous that drivers abandoned their cars in the streets. It was estimated that about 4,000 people died prematurely in the immediate aftermath and as many as another 4,000 to 8,000 more may have perished from lingering longer-term effects.

MORNING SMOG IN SHANGHAI, CHINA.

In January of 1969 the worst maritime oil spill, to that time, took place six miles off the coast of Santa Barbara, California. It was then and there that an oil drilling platform explosion released an estimated 100,000 barrels of crude oil, over an eleven-day period, into the ocean, killing untold numbers of birds and marine wildlife and contaminating pristine beaches for 35 miles. Later, during the early days of the environmental movement, President Nixon, who was from California, reflected upon the disaster saying, "It is said that it was necessary that Santa Barbara should be the example that had to bring it to the attention of the American people." Probably the one event most exemplifying the magnitude of the problem and the state of the environment at that time was that which occurred in June of 1969, when the Cuyahoga River in Cleveland, Ohio, caught fire. But that was hardly the first time the river caught fire. Dating back to the beginning of that century, the river actually caught fire on several other occasions. In fact, the iconic photo of the Cuyahoga River Fire, which appeared in *Time* magazine a month after the fire of 1969 and sparked a public outcry, was of a much more severe fire on the same river that occurred in 1952.

Some of you may recall the "Keep America Beautiful" environmental ads of the time, particularly the "Crying Indian" ad of 1970 that was so emotionally impactful for many. If it was before your time, or even if not, please watch it on YouTube to get a sense or to refresh your memory as to how far we have come in little less than fifty years. What you may not recall, even if you are old enough, and it may come as a surprise regardless of your age and recollection, is that it was Richard M. Nixon who signed the Executive Order on July 9, 1970 that established the Environmental Protection Agency (EPA). Since that time and through the efforts of a multitude of organizations and entities, significant progress has been made in restoring the vast majority of the waterways in the United States. So measurable the improvement in fact that, although once seemingly impossible, populations of native fish have now come back to many of these waterways. Air quality, too, has much improved in U.S. urban centers. NYC has not seen a major smog event of any significance since the 1970s, and today ozone levels in Los Angeles are at 40% of those recorded in 1970. At the same time as these reductions came about, the number of cars on the roadways nearly doubled. Probably most symbolic of our environmental achievements since the 1960s is that in 1995 the bald eagle was removed from the Endangered Species List.

While it may be true that considerable and significant improvements have been made on the environmental front for the majority of the developed world, it is also true that there is more that can and should be done. After all, recall the Mississippi River in the United States and the Sarno River in Italy cited previously are still among the world's ten most polluted rivers. Unfortunately, as with most bureaucracies, the EPA has lost its way. It now focuses on far too many superfluous punitive regulations driven by very vocal fringe extremist organizations. The result is excessive layering of regulation having only marginal impact if any and even in some cases being counterproductive or having undesirable unintended consequences. While not under the purview of the EPA, there has been some recent "feel good" legislation enacted by several municipalities that has received considerable publicity. One of the most notable are the recent bans on plastic shopping bags and plastic straws in California and Washington ,DC, as well as other municipalities, nationally and worldwide. Initiatives such as this, while well-intentioned and logical in their simplicity, are unfortunate diversions in that they are the vehicle for politicians to redirect focus from the bigger and more difficult problems that they wish to avoid. There are an estimated eight million tons of plastics that end up in the world's oceans each year, and although there is no reliable data on what portion of that eight million is from plastic straws, it is surely a negligible fraction thereof. The "feel good" legislation may be nice for those who take comfort from it, but it's not hard to understand that far greater impact on the global problem could be achieved with some effort directed to clean-up of the Ganges, Citarum, and Yellow Rivers, or maybe a little closer to home, and under the jurisdiction of the EPA, the Mississippi River. When it comes to actionable priorities, with all the environmental hysteria out there, when was the last time you were aware of any activist or politician having expressed any concern for or cited any planed action to address the environmental condition of the Mississippi?

Just a few years ago, while living in Southern California, I was greeted by a representative of Greenpeace outside a shopping center. He and his companion (a young woman) both glowed with a wholesome idealistic passion for the cause for which they were soliciting donations. Although skeptical by nature, I was drawn to them as I am often drawn to purchasing cookies from Girl Scouts in similar circumstances. After all these were not the homeless who were becoming more frequent occupiers of public spaces such as this in much of California at that time. It came as no surprise that he was eager to explain their cause, which was simple enough, and it also came with little surprise that they were seeking donations to support their cause. Specifically, they were soliciting funds to support habitats for certain endangered species indigenous to California. There were only a few that they were focused on saving, but I had never heard of any, and I reluctantly admit that they failed to make enough of an impression to allow me to recall today what they were. Consistent with my nature, I was honest with the young man, advising him that I was not particularly familiar with the plight of the particular species they were desirous of saving. His response was hardly a surprise either when he asked why that should have any bearing on my decision to donate to the cause? Which, he went on to assure me, was indeed a good one. I acknowledged my confidence in his belief in the merit of their cause but went on to advise him that I rarely gave to anything unless I believed that I at least had a reasonable understanding of it. Moreover, I informed him that I also did not believe that extinction was a particularly bad thing. After all it is a quite natural occurrence in the history of evolution. In fact, of all the creatures that have at one time or another inhabited the earth, the vast majority are now extinct. I went on to rhetorically question him about his feelings toward the extinction of the dinosaurs, and I admitted that although it's not something I generally give much thought to, I do have an aversion toward wild animals that could, and very well would like to, eat me. I for one find solace in the fact that the dinosaurs are extinct, and I am reasonably confident that even the most liberal of Californians are thankful that saber-tooth tigers are no longer roaming the Hollywood Hills.

Chapter 6

Politics

"Government is not reason; it is not eloquent; it is force. Like fire, it is a dangerous servant and fearful master."

—George Washington

When it comes to politics, few things perplex me more than when one persuasion takes a self-righteous condescending tone in accusing their opposition of "politicizing" an issue. After all, do we actually have an expectation that a politician would do anything but politicize an issue for which there is not universal acceptance and agreement? How does this, and how is it allowed to, persist without challenge? How do we engender substantive discussions and/or debate on issues? Our form of a democratic, representative government, more or less, presumes that our elected officials, seeking re-election, act in accordance with the desires of their constituency. Simply put, logic would seemingly dictate that any publicly elected official would be motivated to act in a manner that would garner the greatest number of votes from the people they represent. So, is the act of, or the accusation of, politicizing an issue reduced to indictments of the representative's constituency? As logical as the unfortunate probability of this would seem to be, it is more likely a simple attempt to stifle discussion and/or debate on a subject. There are several issues that fully fall in the purview of our elected officials' responsibilities to address and represent a clear and present danger to the "General Welfare" of American citizens, but they get little attention. I will cite just two of the most obvious and notable:

- ❖ The National Debt exceeding $20 trillion and continuing to grow.
- ❖ The Solvency of Social Security, Medicaid, and Medicare.

Instead of receiving the necessary attention and sense of urgency that both these issues merit, other issues of little consequence to the "**General** Welfare" of the citizenry have consumed considerably more attention and energies by both public officials and the press alike. Most of which seemingly have come to prominence from nowhere and for which it is difficult to understand the basis for any attention at all, except maybe for very small segments of the population. Two that in recent years have been built up to stir passions to a fever pitch for much broader groups of the population have been:

- ❖ Transgender public restrooms.
- ❖ Civil War Confederate memorials and statues.

The possibility that subjects such as these should be reaching prominence beyond that of maybe some small and localized constituency is seemingly illogical, nonsensical, and irrational. But why, and how? Is it a loss of virtue amongst our elected leaders, apathy, and/or ignorance of the electorate, or is it just that things overall are so good and we have become so consumed by our daily lives that we are enabling our elected officials to take a path of least resistance? Are we allowing them to feed us strawmen as fodder for the most vocal extremist, so they have something to whine about in their leisure? Most likely it's a combination of all the above, enabled and compounded by the dereliction of the one entity necessary to keep the government in check, priorities in order, and to feed the electorate with concise, reliable, and germane information. Journalism and the press, collectively the mass media, in recent years have devolved into little more than sensationalistic tabloids and propaganda machines, propagating bad or patently false information and promoting public apathy through their misinformation and loss of credibility. The necessity of a free and vibrant press is so profound and essential to a working democracy it is codified in the First Amendment of the constitution. Unfortunately, it is currently failing us, and, interestingly enough, this is not the first time in the short history of the United States. So critical the issue, and so exhaustive the subject matter to explore, it could easily consume the entirety of a full book on the topic. Quite ironically a work has recently been published that indeed explores the subject in depth, I will therefore simply refer you to Mark Levin's latest book appropriately titled: *Unfreedom of the Press*.

The base reality is that today and for many decades now we have had the luxury of being able to be complacent. When the national debt reaches a limit whereupon it can no longer be sustained and economic collapse is imminent or worse has arrived and/or when Social Security, Medicaid, and Medicare are indeed no longer solvent, the political will and capital necessary to address each of them will accordingly be found.

Of all the notable quotes made through the years by U.S. Presidents there are a handful that in their time were truly great and continue to stand the test of time. And this was indeed the case when in 1933 Franklin Delano Roosevelt, at his first inaugural, said that "The Only Thing We Have to Fear, is Fear Itself," there was surely plenty to be fearful of. The United States, in fact most of the developed world, was in the midst of a Great Depression, Adolf Hitler and the Nazi party were coming into power in Germany, and there was the rise Mussolini in Italy and other fascists in Europe. In Asia, Japan was flexing its muscle with their initial invasion of Manchuria in 1931. Roosevelt's most immediate concern of course was a domestic one, specifically the economic depression in the U.S., and to this regard he had the understanding and presence of mind to realize that the underlying problem was a lack of confidence. Moreover, he had the intestinal fortitude and leadership qualities that drove him to speak the simple truth about what was so plainly obvious to him and others in his administration. He went on through his nearly four terms as president to face an endless litany of monumental challenges by simply confronting and aggressively working each problem. Certainly, his approach to many of the issues he faced can be and are debated, but then many indeed were fiercely debated in Congress at the time and, moreover, challenged in the press, although for the most part he enjoyed general support from journalists. In retrospect, it should be readily obvious that the political process and media of the day had served us well through such trying times, and indeed as things turned out, it was proven retrospectively, that the only thing we [had] to fear [was] fear itself.

Today, in comparison, we live in the most prosperous of times in all of human history, and by considerable measure. Yet it is not uncommon, in fact it is very common, to see politicians stand at the podium doing the exact opposite of FDR, stoking fear and telling us how ghastly awful the state of affairs now are and how wretched and evil their opposition is. They will stand up and repeatedly tell us that they will fight the good fight, for us, against their opposition who are trying to oppress and exploit us; not only do they attack the candidate in opposition to them, but they also target those voting for their opponent. It is not uncommon to hear attacks along the lines of, my opponent is supported by a "basket full of deplorables" or those misogynistic, racist, homophobic, xenophobes. Another relatively more specific and favorite target is the "wealthy," rarely defined other than some loose references to the "one-percenters." And why not? Historically, class warfare has generally worked well, if not for the proletariat, certainly for those espousing and promoting it — at least in the short term. After all, it's simple math that even a politician can do. You simply surrender or more accurately sacrifice 1% of the vote by vilifying them in your pursuit of acquiring the other 99%. In reality, the promotion of class warfare is nothing more than an attempt to stimulate and leverage the primal emotion of envy. Even in Alexander Hamilton's day he noted the nefarious nature of such arguments, when in 1789 he wrote in a letter to the New York State Electors. "There is no stronger sign of combinations unfriendly to the general good, than when the partisans of those in power raise an indiscriminate cry against men of property."

Most prolific is the statement that the wealthy don't pay their fair share in taxes. And how is "fair share" defined? It generally isn't, but it sounds good in its deliberate ambiguity and its purposeful intent to mislead. The fact is that ever since Federal income taxes were first levied, briefly during the Civil War and later in the 1900s, becoming a permanent source of revenue in 1913 when the 16th Amendment to the Constitution was ratified, the wealthy have carried most of the burden. Rather than argue the semantics of what represents a fair share, I will provide the following statistics from the 2016 tax year for your consideration.

- ❖ The top 50% of all taxpayers paid 97% of all individual income taxes, while the bottom 50% paid the remaining 3%.

- ❖ The top 1% paid a greater share of the individual income taxes (paying 37.3%) than the bottom 90% combined (paying 30.5%).

❖ The top 1% of taxpayers paid an average 26.9% individual income tax rate, which is more than seven times higher than taxpayers in the bottom 50%, who paid an average 3.7%.

The above data is all relative to taxes on income, but even if you could
seize all the wealth of the top 1%, roughly estimated to be about $5
trillion, it wouldn't be enough to pay off 25% of our current debt, and it
would be barely enough to finance our government for one year. Moreover, the seizure of that wealth is an illusion, since most of it is held or
invested in capital assets, not piles of cash in a bank or in heaping piles
on the beds of the wealthy that they roll around in each evening. Of
these assets the vast majority are held in the form of shares of publicly
traded companies. Any mass attempt to liquidate these equity positions
would result in the failure of the companies, and thereby the loss of
jobs and the income of millions. It is not so much that the very wealthy
actually "have" vast wealth, rather they "control" vast wealth. The real
question in this context is who do we want controlling this wealth? In
the case of Amazon, in lieu of Jeff Bezos, do you believe it would be
fairer to turn control of the company over to Alexandria Ocasio-Cortez?
Would social welfare be better served if the Bill & Melinda Gates Foundation was confiscated from Bill and Melinda to be brought under the
control of Bill and Hillary and the Clinton Global Initiative? And surely
Chuck Schumer and Nancy Pelosi could better manage and redirect the
massive assets and investments that make up the portfolio of Berkshire
Hathaway than could Warren Buffet.

Another ploy is to cite extremes in income and/or wealth inequality and
blur distinctions between the two or to simply state that all the money is
in the hands of the wrong people. And the solution, to demonize capitalism and propose schemes for income redistribution through socialistic

government programs. But capitalism is not the problem, it's the solution. Historically, it's the great equalizer of income inequality. Take for example George Washington, who in his time was one of the wealthiest, if not the wealthiest of our founders, owning sizable portions of Virginia and large tracts of land in the Ohio River valley. That concentration of wealth did not stay intact very long after his death. Can you even put a finger on how and to whom it was redistributed? One thing is for sure, it was with no assistance by the government. Moreover, there wasn't even an income tax in his day. And what of the wealth of the great industrialists or "robber barons;" J.P. Morgan, John D. Rockefeller, and Andrew Carnegie, etc.? Other than the many philanthropic foundations they established, little of those great concentrations of wealth lasted beyond a few generations.

In addition to the focus on specific cases of extreme wealth, the focus on an increase in a wealth gap in recent years has also become an attractive distraction. While it is true that in more recent years there has indeed been an increase, it is nothing new, and the market will make adjustments accordingly without the outside influences of government. When adjusted to current dollars, industrialists John D. Rockefeller and Cornelius Vanderbilt had a net worth of more than $250 billion and $200 billion respectively, while the median income in their time was about $16,000/year in today's dollars. Compared to the wealthiest American today, Jeff Bezos with an estimated net worth of $165 billion, and a current median income of about $53,000/year, one could easily argue that the wealth gap is in fact significantly less than it was 100 years ago. Much of the argument being made regarding any increase in a wealth gap is based upon the cherry-picking of statistical data, and I acknowledge that the same could be said for what has been presented here in the foregoing comparison of Rockefeller, Vanderbilt, and Bezos. Indeed, any comparison to 1% or less of a general population is going to be a comparison to an aberration of that population.

The recent increase in the gap of wealth distribution began in the 1980s and has continued increasing with the rise of the tech industry, falling dramatically with the dot-com bust at the end of the 1990s into the 2000s and resuming with more recent prosperity. Several reasons for this could be cited, but it is this author's belief that it is basically a function of the nature of the tech industry in conjunction with an increase in multinationalism and international trade. Simply put, the tech industry requires far less capital and labor investments than that which was required in other sectors and during earlier industrial periods. In conjunction with the drastically lower costs of readily accessible and reliable overseas production, they combine to produce much higher asset valuations for their stakeholders.

At this point we need to ask the question, has our political process, and as an extension the political climate, really devolved to the dire state that it readily appears to the casual observer? Even the question itself seems to presuppose that it indeed has. If we assume the term "casual observer" represents the average American outside of the establishment or groupthink of those vested and immersed in it, people focused on the day-to-day aspects of their lives with only a peripheral view of the circus events taking place inside the beltway, then it would be logical that the average American has only their life experience and exposure as a framework to draw a comparison from. Moreover, the downward spiral of political discourse in recent years has in all likelihood driven the average American to move even farther from the sidelines, making their casual observations even more distant. The fact is that politics has always been a very nasty business, although I admit I'm finding it difficult to identify historical parallels to the climate in which the Trump Administration currently operates. The closest may be that of Andrew Jackson, who is addressed later in this chapter.

In the first administration, even under the leadership of George Washington, partisan positions were fiercely fought based upon strongly held and opposing ideologies, most notably those held by Thomas Jefferson, the first Secretary of State, and Alexander Hamilton, the first Secretary of the Treasury. Later these battles would bleed over into a three-way tryst that included John Adams, the first Vice President, who went on to become the second President of the United States.

The Hamilton side:

❖ Leanings and a preference toward better relations and alliances with England over France.

❖ Belief in a relatively strong Federal Government, drawn upon Hamilton and Washington's experience with a weak Continental Congress during the Revolutionary War.

❖ The foundation of the U.S. economy viewed in terms of it being based upon commerce, manufacturing, banking, and a vision of future industrialization.

❖ Referred to as the "Federalists."

The Jefferson side:

❖ Leanings and a preference toward better relations and alliances with France over England.

❖ Belief in a relatively small, comparatively weak Federal Government, secondary to that of the individual States.

❖ The foundation of the U.S. economy viewed in terms of it being based upon an Agrarian Society.

❖ Referred to initially as the "Anti-Federalists" and later as the "Democratic Republicans" (Republications for short, but no relationship to today's Republican Party).

These men held their ideologies in high esteem and fought for them publicly and privately with an abundance of passion. In his first administration, George Washington, who for the most part held himself above the fray, regularly found he was caught up in mediating disputes between the two, with each of them regularly jockeying for his favor behind the back of the other. Much like politicians of today, direct public confrontation between the two was avoided; instead, furious public battles played out through unabashed openly partisan print news. Hamilton's proxy was the *Gazette of the United States* edited by John Fenno, and for Jefferson, and by extension his surrogate James Madison, it was the *National Gazette* edited by Philip Freneau. Both publications shamelessly hurdled partisan and slanderous accusations, attacking their opposition with unsubstantiated allegations from anonymous sources, including, but not limited to, claims of supporting monarchy, embezzlement, and collusion with foreign powers (the latter having recently been replayed over a three-year period by the modern press). It may come as a surprise for readers today to know that these publications, not unlike many of their day, were openly partisan, making no pretense of neutrality. At least their readers were of no illusion regarding the slant and substance of what they were reading. Even Jefferson whose actions played an active role, although always under cover of surrogates, began to acknowledge the beast he had a hand in feeding when he stated, "Nothing can now be believed which is seen in a newspaper," and "Truth itself becomes suspicious by being put into that polluted vehicle." Could Jefferson be implying that the press of his day was becoming an "enemy of the people?"

In 1797, the first sex scandal in American history was played out in the press. The subject of the scandal was Alexander Hamilton himself, and quite apart from much of the print of that period, this scandal had some basis in fact. The affair with Maria Reynolds was held as a well-guarded secret for more than four years, but when gossip began to leak in association with allegations disparaging his service as Treasury Secretary, his honor was in jeopardy. Interestingly enough, the object of Hamilton's concern and focus was more on his dealings and reputation as Treasury Secretary and less on the affair. His response was to publish a letter in the *Gazette of the United States*, stating that the charges of misdeeds or even illegal dealings as Treasury Secretary were false and misleading but acknowledging the affair with Mrs. Reynolds. This only served to give the scandal even more traction, which was further exploited by the *Aurora*, another proxy of Jefferson and Madison. In an effort to squelch the burgeoning sensationalistic story, Hamilton took a surprising and truly amazing action to refute the claims by publishing a pamphlet detailing the facts and many of the titillating details related to the stories. Based upon Hamilton's account of the events that took place, it was Maria Reynolds who came to him seeking financial assistance, claiming that she and her young daughter were abandoned by her husband, James Reynolds, and left destitute. The affair began when Hamilton went to her boarding house intent on assisting her in her financial plight, whereupon he became engaged in matters other than financial aid. Hamilton subsequently received correspondence from the estranged husband, James Reynolds, demanding $1,000 (roughly $25,000 in today's money) to remain silent about the relationship. Hamilton paid the money and broke off the affair, but this is where the story gets really scurrilous. James then encourages Hamilton to resume the affair, seeking to continue the extortion under the guise of loans from Hamilton. Irrespective of the fact that Hamilton did not comply with Mr. Reynolds' requests, this scandal dealt Hamilton's political future a fatal blow. Unlike Hamilton, Jefferson proved himself much more capable in concealing his relationship with Sally Hemmings for most of his public life.

For the election of 1800, the political assaults by Jefferson and Hamilton turned from each other to become an uncoordinated ambush on the incumbent John Adams. This was striking on both accounts for very different but also very profound reasons. Jefferson, who was then Vice President with divergent political views from Adams (Jefferson a Republican, and Adams a Federalist), was a long-time close friend of both John and Abigail Adams. John Adams was a mentor to the young Jefferson in the early days of the Revolution, and Abigail in earlier times contemplated the possibilities of romance between their son, John Quincy, and Jefferson's daughter, "Patsy." But that was then, and leading up to the election of 1800, resentment and bitterness grew as Jefferson worked behind the scenes to replace Adams in the presidency. So bitter was Adams's resentment of Jefferson that he did not attend his inauguration, leaving the capital that morning at 4:00 a.m. As for the relationship between Hamilton and Adams, dissension seemed always to exist between the two, arising mostly from a clash of their personalities. However, the irony here was that for the most part they were both generally aligned ideologically (both men were Federalists). The political maneuverings by Jefferson and Hamilton did keep Adams from serving a second term, but yielded a tie in electoral votes between Jefferson and an "up-and-comer" by the name of Aaron Burr. In the end even Hamilton preferred Jefferson, as someone having "wrong principles," over Burr, who was someone "devoid of principles." With a tie in the Electoral College the decision as to who would become president was passed to the House of Representatives, and on the 36th vote the House selected Thomas Jefferson to become the third President of the United States, with Aaron Burr becoming the Vice President. An additional outcome of this election was that the seeds of animosity and resentment by Burr toward Hamilton were now sewn and would ultimately lead to the death of Hamilton only four years later.

On the morning of July 7, 1804, Hamilton left the docks of New York City at 5:00 a.m. and was rowed across the Hudson River to Weehawken, New Jersey. After weeks of negotiations, the Seconds of Hamilton and Burr were unable to mediate a compromise, and the duel was on. To this day it is still unclear as to exactly what "despicable" accusation Hamilton made about Burr that led to this "affair of honor." According to Ron Chernow in his book titled *Hamilton*, "Burr was such a dissipated, libidinous character that Hamilton had a rich field to choose from in assailing his personal reputation. Aaron Burr had been openly accused of every conceivable sin: deflowering virgins, breaking up marriages through adultery, forcing women into prostitution, accepting bribes, fornicating with slaves, and looting the estates of legal clients." We may never know of the specifics leading to this affair, but what we do know is that at 7:00 a.m. that morning the two exchanged salutations, then at a distance of ten paces, Alexander Hamilton, the nation's first Secretary of the Treasury, faced Aaron Burr, the third Vice President of the United States, for what would turn out to be the last time. Although we will never know for sure, as eyewitness accounts conflict, it is most likely that Hamilton threw away his shot, by firing first and deliberately missing Burr. Then Burr, taking deliberate aim, fired within seconds, mortally wounding Hamilton. Later, Henry Adams would refer to the event as "the most dramatic moment in the early politics of the Union."

A PERIOD REPRESENTATION OF THE DUEL BETWEEN AARON BURR AND ALEXANDER HAMILTON.

Of contests such as this, and the nature of politics in their day, Ron Chernow said, "Politicians were the most ardent duelists. Political parties were still fluid organizations based on personality cults, and no politician could afford to have his honor impugned. Though fought in secrecy and seclusion, duels always turned into highly public events that were covered afterward with rapt attention by the press. They were designed to sway public opinion and shape the images of the adversaries." Maybe if the practice were to be resurrected and legalized today (for the political class and journalist alike), some semblance of civility could be restored to our political discourse. Just a thought.

Arguably the most contentious election in American history, and certainly the most slanderous and bitterly fought, was that of 1828 between Andrew Jackson and incumbent John Quincy Adams. While much of the mudslinging that took place leading up to this election, and continued for much of the Jackson presidency, makes the current political climate seem to pale somewhat in comparison, there are some striking similarities and parallels that can be drawn between the environment and players today and their counterparts 190 years ago. John Quincy Adams, who was the son of the second President John Adams, was viewed as an "establishment" candidate. Seemingly groomed for the job, he was a man with arguably the best pedigree and resume of anyone to serve as an American president. As an adolescent and young man, he traveled with his father to Europe and was by his side for much of his father's international diplomacy during the revolutionary period. Educated at Harvard, he was appointed ambassador to the Netherlands by President Washington, and later to Russia and then Prussia under subsequent administrations and was part of the American delegation that negotiated the end of the War of 1812 with Great Britain. Andrew Jackson, who was viewed as a "populist" candidate, was orphaned at the age of 14 when his mother died of cholera. Mostly self-educated, he was known to be somewhat of a tempestuous frontiersman, found of whisky, women, horses, gambling, and dueling; he later settled in Tennessee, becoming a lawyer. He came to national prominence during the War of 1812, principally for his defense of New Orleans in a battle where his leadership proved superior to a British force that outnumbered his own by almost two to one. When the smoke cleared, the British were turned back, with the Americans suffering 333 casualties to the British 2,459 casualties.

The seeds for this brutal presidential contest were sewn four years earlier when Jackson won a plurality of the popular vote at 42% and 99 of the electoral votes, which was more than any other candidate, but still short of the 131 votes needed for a true majority. The decision then went to the House of Representatives, who selected John Quincy over Jackson to become the sixth President of the United States, setting the stage for the election that would follow four years later in 1828. Years before the election, the slanderous accusations and mud began to fly from the followers, surrogates, and partisan newspapers supporting each of the candidates. Adams was referred to as "lordly, purse-proud," and an aristocrat "feeding at the public trough," citing, of all things, a billiard table he purchased for the White House. As if that were not enough, he was also accused of having premarital relations with his wife and called a "pimp" for allegedly procuring young girls for the exploits of Czar Alexander while serving as a minister to Russia. Jackson was called a drunkard, a duelist and a cockfighter, a man who could not even spell the word "Europe." His wife, Rachel, was assailed and labeled an "adulteress," "a polygamist" and even a "whore." She died of a heart attack shortly after the election, but before her husband took office. For the remainder of his life Jackson blamed his adversaries for her death. Although at her funeral he said, "In the presence of this dear saint, I can and do forgive all my enemies. But those vile wretches who have slandered her must look to God for mercy."

Two final notes on Jackson: at his death he still had two bullets lodged in his body from duels he engaged in earlier in his life, and in a failed assassination attempt on his life, when both pistols of his attacker misfired, the infuriated Jackson countered the attack by beating the would-be assassin to near death with his cane.

POLITICAL FIGHTS – A crude portrayal of a fight on the floor of Congress between Vermont Representative Matthew Lyon and Roger Griswold of Connecticut.

In the years leading up to the American Civil War, the vile and slanderous rhetoric was building in the growing divide between the two bitterly opposed factions. On May 22, 1856, in the United States Senate, it came to a crescendo when Representative Charles Sumner (R-MA), a staunch abolitionist, was nearly beaten to death by the cane of Representative Preston Brooks (D-SC). The day just prior, Senator Sumner gave a speech in which he assailed the "murderous robbers from Missouri," calling them "hirelings, picked from the drunken spew and vomit of an uneasy civilization." He went on referring to a fellow senator of the opposition as an "imbecile" having "chosen a mistress. I mean the harlot, slavery." A senator from Illinois, Stephen Douglas, was heard to have said of Sumner, "That damn fool will get himself killed by some other damn fool." Subsequent to the beating, Senator Brooks was levied a fine of $300 and resigned his post in the Senate. He returned to South Carolina where he was hailed for his actions and was later reelected for another term. Upon his return to the Senate, he was sent canes from all over the south to replace the one he broke on Sumner.

As tensions continued to build in the young republic, it was becoming clear that things would ultimately play out as Carl von Clausewitz famously said, "War is merely a continuation of politics by other means." Clearly democracy had its limits, and those limits were being tested in increasingly dangerous ways. The founders were very cognizant of these limitations, as many had studied the early Greek republics, drawing what attributes they could from them and attempting to address the obvious flaws. At this point you may be asking, but what flaws could exist in a democracy? After all, one man, one vote, right? They were challenging themselves to find a delicate balance wherein they could counterbalance a maximum of individual freedom from the potentially oppressive will of a majority. For them the utopian solution would be no government at all, but as Madison wrote in Federalist #51, "If men were angels, no government would be necessary," and the founders were of no illusion about the virtues of man. Paramount of the flaws with which they struggled and were most concerned about was what they referred to as the potential for "Tyranny of the Majority," which was masterly defined by Benjamin Franklin when he said:

> "Democracy is two wolves and one lamb voting on what to have for dinner."

Similarly, John Adams wrote on the perils of majority rule:

> "Absolute power in a majority is as drunk as it is in one."

It was in part due to the pervasive perils they perceived from their studies of questions such as these that they came to compromise on the imperative resolutions that yielded the Electoral College and a bicameral Legislature (House of Representatives, and the Senate).

Among the many compromises that were achieved in formulating and then ratifying the Constitution of the United States, one of the most essential is now broadly looked back upon with vile contempt. As controversial as it may be viewed in retrospect today, overlooking the worldwide morays of their day, the compromise arrived upon to address the issue of slavery was nonetheless essential in founding the new republic. Although never addressed directly within the constitution, it was perhaps one of their more amazing achievements from a purely political perspective, although today it is rarely regarded as such. Unfortunately, today the view of this compromise is at best blurred and at worst totally obscured by a pervasive modern-day, simplistic, and self-righteous moralistic judgement. Most often it is conveniently brushed off as a failure by the founders to resolve one of the major issues of their day. But this view is shortsighted on the realities of the extreme division that existed on the subject, as well as the historical fact that the institution of slavery was still widely present throughout the rest of world at the formation of the Union. In the late 1700s there was no option for a compromise that would yield a Federal Union of the States without slavery. It was in essence a purely binary choice: a Federal Union of the States in which approximately half practiced slavery or thirteen Independent States in which approximately half practiced slavery. For the founders it was never a question of whether or not there would be slavery; the question was would there or would there not be a Union of the States. People today lack an appreciation of how very fragile the Union of the States actually was from the period of the founding up to the Civil War, which turned out to be as extreme a test as man could devise. Before the Civil War people generally referred to the Union as "These" United States, whereas after the war it was and continues to typically be referred to as "The" United States. Put in terms of a modern-day issue that resembles a similar near-equal split of opinion and an extreme of opposing passions is the subject of abortion. After decades of hyper-debate, it remains an issue still separated by no more than nine months, and the extreme sentiments on each side remain nowhere near any resolution or compromise, and yet the Union continues (How will future generations a hundred or a hundred and fifty years from now look back upon our present-day divide over abortion? Which side will be tearing down the statues then?).

In his day, Thomas Jefferson characterized slavery best when he said, "We have the wolf by the ears, and we can neither hold him, nor safely let him go." Therefore, to think of this compromise in terms of anything less than groundbreaking for its time is either delusional or disingenuous. It does persist, however, for either a lack of appreciation for the monumental nature of what was achieved and/or a lack of understanding of the context of the time and conditions under which it was achieved, or the alternative, a deliberate effort to defraud others who are lacking in this fundamental understanding. A fact that falls upon many a deaf ear to those who proclaim that the United States was "founded upon slavery" is that, at its founding, the United States led most of the world in the abolition of slavery. Shortly after the founding of the United States, slavery was illegal in nearly half the States, whereas it persisted in much of Europe and the rest of the world, including France and England, for decades well into the early 1800s. Looking back upon history, from the earliest Middle Eastern cultures, through the Egyptians, Greeks, and Romans, up into the 1800s, we find that moral judgements on the institution of slavery are more a reflection upon humanity throughout the ages, and certainly not a function of the founding of the United States. Each society defined the word "Civilization" and what it meant to be civilized based upon the morays of their time and culture. The United States was not founded upon slavery! Quite the contrary, it was a first step in all of humanity toward the abolition of slavery and redefining what it means to be civilized.

Today by contrast, unless faced with truly existential issues, such as the 9/11 attack, the political environment is one in which placating the electorate continues to thrive. It is as true today as when it was observed by Hamilton in his time, and he wrote in a letter to Robert Morris, "The inquiry constantly is what will please, not what will benefit the people. In such a government there can be nothing but temporary expedient, ficklessness, and folly."

Moving from some of the many disconcerting events and issues cited in the foregoing narrative, I will return to the perspective that apart from the flaws in our representative government, it is still far better than any man could endeavor to produce. As Winston Churchill once said of democracy: "It is the worst form of Government except for all the others that have been tried." So then, what of the others? As noted in Chapter 4, the other three major alternatives, communism, socialism, and fascism, are heavily intertwined with or codependent with economic constructs. But in this chapter, I will attempt to isolate the political component of each.

❖ Communism — A naturally totalitarian state by necessity since the government is controlled by a single authoritarian party. Inherent to communism are pervasive limitations in personal freedoms, particularly with respect to property which is owned in common by the state.

❖ Socialism — Although not necessarily totalitarian, the state is authoritarian in its administration of regulation and/or taxation as coercion and force to control production and distribution of goods and services, otherwise property can be privately held.

❖ Fascism — A nationalistic state in which a dictatorial leader of an autocratic government pursues policy in support of cultural and often racial uniformity over individual liberties. It often practices severe economic and social regimentation and forcible suppression of any opposition.

One common feature of all three is that in practice they are and have been authoritarian in nature, limiting personal freedoms to various degrees. In addition to the limitations on personal freedom and property rights, they have, throughout history, also been most notable for some of their tyrannical leaders (dictators) and the masses who perished through their actions. Most notable of course was Adolf Hitler, who is attributed responsibility for more than 15 million civilian deaths, but two others are attributed even greater body counts: Stalin at more than 20 million, and Mao Zedong at more than 40 million. There is indeed considerable variation and debate over statistics such as these, particularly when it comes to what differentiates a civilian fatality from a casualty of war. From the available variations of data, I believe these numbers are most likely conservative representations of the actual orders of magnitude. But then as Joseph Stalin was credited for saying, "A single death is a tragedy; a million deaths is a statistic." Although Stalin may have intended his words to have an alternative meaning, the reality, and regardless of the accuracy of these statistics, is that it remains undeniable that their atrocities were grotesque in both their nature and magnitude. Unfortunately, if his words were intended to be prophetic, he was correct in one regard: that our collective understanding of these acts, and the circumstances leading to them, has faded as the years have passed.

The world today remains populated with a multitude of despots, most notably in the Middle East, Asia, Latin America, and Africa. Although not attributed with mass murder of the magnitude attributed to the three megalomaniacs cited above, the evil they perpetrate is no less wretched. Let us not overlook the colorful character who became the third president of Uganda. Idi Amin Dada is a vivid reminder of the evil that still lurks in the dark reaches of our modern world, when the governed become the subjects of a tyrannical government and/or leader. I use Idi Amin as a representative example, not for his body count, which is estimated to have been 100,000 to 500,000 from a population of little more than 10 million during his rule, but because the images of his despotic exploits are vividly captured by Forest Whitaker in the movie *The Last King of Scotland*. Although the film is a very loose adaptation of historical events, it nonetheless captures the essence of how a young, impressionable, well-educated idealist is susceptible to evil realities that are difficult for him to comprehend. Even today, hidden from world view, the Chinese government holds hundreds of thousands of political dissidents and religious minorities in what they term "re-education" camps. Yet much of the youth in the developed world have a limited awareness of these realities, leaving their impressionable idealism susceptible to utopian socialistic teachings and propaganda.

There are almost as many definitions of the American Dream as there are people willing to define it for use. For most people throughout history and in many places today around the world, their dreams remain simple enough: to not go hungry, to have shelter, to provide for their children, and to not be oppressed and/or exploited by others. In America and most of the developed world, we are fortunate enough to dream well beyond those simple basics. In fact, the reality is that the American Dream is whatever you wish it to be, but let us not forget that in a truly free society the fulfillment of those dreams is in your own hands and not dependent upon the leave of others. Any dependency requires the sacrifice of some freedoms. The only rights a rational person should reasonably expect or desire from their government are those endowed by our creator and put to pen by Thomas Jefferson when he wrote "that among these are Life, Liberty, and the pursuit of Happiness." In other words, it is a fundamental right to be afforded opportunity; what you do with it is fundamentally up to you.

Chapter 7

Religion and Education

"If you don't know where you're going, any road will take you there."

—*George Harrison*

There are few aspects of humanity that are a better indicator of our prosperity and well-being than religion. Unfortunately, it is generally a reverse correlation, in that people tend to flock to their God or become more devout in times of hardship and/or suffering and forsake divinity or become more secular in times of prosperity and/or well-being. This can readily be seen in the narrow context of our everyday lives. As people age and near their own mortality, there is a general tendency to be drawn toward worship more regularly than during any other period of their lives. During times of major catastrophes, such as earthquakes, hurricanes, tornados, or other events generally characterized as being wrought by the Wrath of God, and in their aftermath, we gather for group prayer and candlelight vigils. Similarly, we seek divinity in times of, or in response to, horrific deeds of mankind, such as mass shootings, terrorism, and war. On the contrary, when was the last time you were witness to, or part of, a group prayer or vigil giving thanks for good health, prosperity, and/or general well-being? One would generally need to go to church for that.

Yes, of course there is the Thanksgiving holiday, the only nationally recognized two-day holiday on our calendars, but then this holiday makes my point as profoundly as I believe any can. Today, it is still altogether common that families gather for Thanksgiving, regardless of religious denomination, around a table, which is sometimes candlelit, and oftentimes joining in group prayer. In truth and reality, in our modern times this holiday, like most others, has evolved to be little more than time off from work. The only differentiator from other holidays being the fact that most people get not just one day off from work but two. Not so long ago things were considerably different; from before the Pilgrims up through the time it was first recognized as a federal holiday during the Lincoln administration, it was given the solemn significance it was due, a vivid indicator of how hard times were then when compared to today.

THE FIRST THANKSGIVING AT PLYMOUTH – This 1914 work by Jennie Augusta Brownscombe, which hangs at Pilgrim Hall Museum in Plymouth, Massachusetts, depicts the reverence early Americans had for this occasion.

It was a time when the abundance of your harvest was the only thing that stood between you and a grimly cold dark winter of starvation and the very real possibility of death for you and those you loved dearly. In those days, the basis for giving such thanks was clearly and vividly understood. The transition from a time when the Thanksgiving holiday was observed with the just reverence it was due, to the casual modern day observance was vividly captured by Norman Rockwell in his 1943 painting appropriately titled *Freedom from Want*. You need not travel back too far in time to find that devotion to one's faith in general was far greater than it is today, and the farther back you go the greater and more widespread that devotion.

It is a commonly held view that this transition to a loss of faith is attributed to the increase of general knowledge and understanding of nature, the universe, and natural forces at work or the advent and embrace of the sciences, starting in the 1700s with the Enlightenment. There may well be some merit in this view, and as recognized by a Franciscan Friar in the 14th century, the simplest explanation is generally the correct one. But just as simple is the fact that through the millennia little has changed in the fundamentals of faith and religion, other than maybe the general shift of most major religions to monotheism thousands of years ago. The multitude of discoveries arising from the sciences over the past few hundred years may offer alternative outlets for faith; however, they have fallen short of overturning any basic tenets of the world's great religions or the faith of their followers in general. Surprisingly however, it has been faith that has crept into the discourse of the sciences in recent times to help support or explain irreconcilable phenomena, and I'm not referring to Creation Science, for which I believe there is a valid application. I am referring here to faith where the belief in a deity has been supplanted by other constructs, such as Aliens or Climate Change; the latter of which has already been addressed in an earlier chapter on the environment. Another force that has depressed religion in recent history has been that of the state. Karl Marx, who referred to religion as the "opium of the people," and later Vladimir Lenin both viewed religion as being counter to their struggle, since they believed that the people should place their hopes and faith in, and give their full devotion to, the State. Therefore, one goal of the former Soviet Union was to supplant religious belief in a deity with a godless devotion to the State. At best, religion in the former Soviet Union was frowned upon and discouraged; at worst, it was brutally oppressed. In spite of the Soviet Government's best efforts, religion in several forms was able to survive the repression, although on the whole the numbers of those practicing faith in a benevolent deity did decline dramatically under Soviet rule. Although the Soviets in the U.S.S.R. did realize moderate success in their efforts to push religion from their communities, attempts in other Socialist governments in Eastern Europe and Latin America experienced little to no success in their efforts to repress the beliefs of their people, particularly in countries where Catholicism was deeply rooted.

In ancient times religion was a much more important part of everyday life for the masses than it is in modern times. In Europe, following the decline and fall of the Roman Empire, Christianity became the dominant religion as humanity entered the Dark Ages, continuing through the Middle Ages. It was omnipresent in the lives of the vast majority of individuals and their communities. During this period, where hardship and suffering reached depths unequaled in other periods of European history, the Roman Catholic Church grew to be the central faith throughout the continent, reaching into all aspects of the population's everyday life and gaining great wealth, political power, and influence over art, architecture, and education. This was an age of faith that set precedents for societies and the many Protestant offshoots that would follow for many years to come. Communities were organized around the local church, which became the center for social services and spiritual guidance. In an age where harsh famine and plague regularly loomed, the church provided the only refuge and prayer, the only potential for deliverance and salvation. This was also the age when the great cathedrals of Europe were constructed. Try to imagine, if you can, the collective extreme of devotion it takes to design and build structures that you know you will never have the opportunity to see completed, and in most cases will not be completed for successive generations to come. As great the symbolism of these structures came to be, the influence of the church was just as pervasive in the arts and education. Since few people of the period could read, much of the art was used as inspirational tools to teach the faith to the masses. The churches' and cathedrals' great stained-glass windows, murals, frescoes, and paintings depicted lessons and teachings of the faith for the common man. Monasteries were the preeminent institutions of higher learning, and monks were the learned men of their time, spending much of their time reading and transcribing scripture, ancient manuscripts, and texts by hand. The dominant hold that the Roman Catholic Church had on Europe did not begin to unravel until the Reformation led by Martin Luther in the early 1500s. The spread of the Protestant faith was made possible by the printing press. Invented less than a hundred years earlier by Gutenberg and first used to spread the faith with the printing of the Bible, it had the unintended consequence of circumventing the stranglehold the Roman Catholic Church had on the dissemination of information by enabling the spread of Protestant beliefs.

LEONARDO DA VINCI'S LAST SUPPER – Housed at the Convent of Santa Maria delle Grazie in Milan, Italy, this work by da Vinci is one of the world's most recognizable. Painted in the 1490s, it told the story of the Last Supper to a widely illiterate populace.

Whether under the Roman Catholic Church or a derivative Protestant denomination, Christianity remained dominant and unchanged in its dominion over the lives of the people throughout Europe and up through the founding of the New World. Contrary to a current growing and increasingly pervasive belief, Christianity was in fact a preeminent force and influence in the founding of the United States. Neither Jefferson, Franklin, nor any of the other founders were ever espousing the formation of a secular state. Up to the revolution, through the founding, and beyond, communities across North America, although predominantly of Protestant faith, very much resembled their predecessors in Europe. Rural villages, towns, and city neighborhoods were organized around their local churches. Very much parallel to the development and evolution of society in Medieval Europe, communities in North America were also structured around the local church, which acted as centers for social services and spiritual guidance. In the early colonies they also took on an additional role, in that they often doubled as governmental and political centers of the congregation. In many communities they became as much the hotbeds to express displeasure and dissent toward the British Crown as did the local taverns. Religious faith, again predominantly Protestant denominations of Christianity, remained a dominant force in the lives of Americans after the revolution and through its first century and well into its second century. Alexus de Tocqueville, a contemporary source on this subject, wrote at length on the role of religion in the fabric of American society in the early 1800s, specifically observing:

> *"Religion in America takes no direct part in the government of society, but it must be regarded as the first of their 'political institutions;' for it does not only impart a 'taste for freedom,' it facilitates the use of it. Indeed, it is in this same point of view that the inhabitants of the United States themselves look upon religious belief. I do not know whether all Americans have a sincere faith in their religion — but I am certain that they hold it to be indispensable to the maintenance of the republican institutions. This opinion is not peculiar to a class of citizens or to a party, but it belongs to the whole nation and to every rank of society..."*

From the time the first pilgrims landed at Plymouth Rock up through the Industrial Revolution, religion, in the form of Protestant Christianity, was a readily apparent component of what it was to be American. Life on this new continent at this time was, at the risk of understating, a daily challenge, and as alluded to in earlier chapters, it required exceptionally hard work and much sacrifice just to survive. Whether on the frontier or in the towns, villages, or cities of America the Christian Faith was very much ubiquitous, and equally present was what came to be known as the "Protestant work ethic," a concept for which an emphasis is placed on hard work, discipline, and frugality, conjoined with a person's adherence to values espoused by the Protestant faith. This was one of those phenomena where the adage "What came first, the chicken or the egg?" is readily applicable. Was it the Protestant Faith that drove the people of that time, or was it the hard work that drove and sustained their faith? Irrespective of what answer you may arrive at, the predominance of faith through those times was readily evident to those who observed it, including Tocqueville who captured it in his writings of the time, even though the phrase "Protestant work ethic" was not coined until years later, in 1905 by Max Weber.

Later, in the 1950s, the relationship of faith with the American culture was reinforced when, in response to the threat of Soviet aggression during the Cold War and the generally held view of the Soviet Union as a "Godless nation," the phrase "under God" was added to the pledge of allegiance in 1954 and "In God We Trust" to our currency in 1957. It was not until the 1960s and the relative prosperity of the times that the relationship between the U.S. Government and organized religion began to change, when in 1962 a ruling by the Supreme Court banned religious observances, such as prayer in public schools. The revisionist interpretation of Jefferson's writings on the "Separation of Church and State" that was brought about by this ruling later led to pressing rigid teachings of Evolution over any Creationist belief in schools. In the years that followed, the tide continued to build with the removal of art that had a religious context, such as the crucifix or Moses and the Ten Commandments, from public buildings and public spaces and the banning of Christmas trees and nativity scenes in public spaces, as well as public and private shaming for using the phrase "Merry Christmas." For a lighthearted, more in depth look into this subject see Ben Stein's film: *Expelled — No Intelligence Allowed.*

Today the countries with the highest percentage of their population having religious faith are found in Africa and Southeast Asia, where, not so coincidently, the highest levels of hardship and/or suffering are also found. Next is the Middle East, where hardship and/or suffering amongst the general population is also very high, although another factor surely is that these countries also tend to have theocratic forms of government, which would also drive up their numbers. In about the middle are most of the South and Central American countries, where hardship and/or suffering levels are more moderate. On the other end of the spectrum are the countries where relatively lower percentages of the population have religious faith and where general prosperity and/or wellbeing is enjoyed; these include the United States, Canada, and Australia, as well as most of those in Europe. China is at the extreme to this end of this spectrum with the lowest percentage of their population having religious faith, and it is an obvious anomaly since its population would hardly be considered prosperous. While there are a number of historical factors that attribute to this, the most notable would be the repression of religion under Mao Zedong. There are a few other anomalies, but for the most part throughout the globe, those populations having the greatest percentage of their population practicing religious faith are those with the highest levels of hardship and/or suffering. And those populations having the lowest percentage of their population practicing religious faith are those with the highest levels of prosperity and/or wellbeing.

Education, unlike religion, would appear to have a direct correlation to the relative prosperity of individuals and their societies as a whole. One contradiction to this line of reasoning is that in very recent decades there has been a growing concern for a perceived decline in the quality of education in the United States, and with some good justification. The responses to which, as with many governmental bureaucratic responses, is a misdirection of focus from the real issues and root causes. Unfortunately, in this case, there is a focus on the equality of education for all, rather than the quality of education for individuals. Similar to the housing bubble of the mid to late 2000s where there was an emphasis placed on home ownership by all, regardless of individual circumstance, and ready access to easy money to support it through government programs and promotion, the same has now been playing out with respect to higher education. In recent decades emphasis has been placed on college educations for all, regardless of individual circumstance, and ready access to easy money to support it through governmental programs and promotion. The net effect, not unlike that which occurred in the housing market, is excessive and unsustainable debt on those who pursued educations they did not complete or if obtained had no marketable use. Except in this case, individuals are now indentured to the government in lieu of private banks. So as is necessary when things such as this go awry and someone or some entity is needed to take the fall, who will they (or we, through our elected representatives) blame? If it cannot be the government programs put into practice, all be it with good intention, it must be a "rigged system." Another unfortunate reality is that even if a satisfactory scapegoat is identified, the problem will still be with us: a decline in education, but now with overly burdensome debt. It is difficult to predict the future outcome of such a trend, particularly based upon such a short period in history, but surely it is not something that could, or for that matter should, promote optimism. Although it is difficult to draw parallels from history, the last time there was a major decline in levels of education would have been during the decline and fall of the Roman Empire, and that didn't work out well for the people of Rome, or the rest of Europe for that matter.

It should come as little surprise that in the aftermath of the fall of Rome, through the Dark Ages and Medieval Europe, the peoples of Europe were by and large illiterate with rare and few exceptions. Education for the general populace who were not tied to farming was in the form of apprenticeships or indentured servitude in the limited number of skilled trades that existed. The little that people had to stimulate their minds, when they were not consumed with the preoccupation of survival, came from the church, visually in the form of art and orally in the form of the spoken gospel or song. Illiteracy rates began to decline in Europe during the Reformation, subsequent to invention of the printing press and availability of the Bible to the masses. It continued to decline slowly but steadily through the 1700s and into the 1800s; however, this decline was mostly limited to the upper classes, with the level of literacy amongst the common folk, for those who obtained it, only being marginal. Interestingly enough, during the same period, literacy in the U.S. was increasing at a rate that was significantly outpacing that of its European counterparts. It is estimated that by the mid-1800s the literacy rate in the U.S. was reaching 80%, outpacing most European nations by 10% to 20%. Alexus de Tocqueville also wrote of his observations on the nature of education in American society of the early 1800s. Specifically noting:

"The observer who is desirous of forming an opinion on the state of instruction amongst the Anglo-Americans must consider the same object from two different points of view. If he only singles

*out the learned, he will be astonished to find how rare they are;
but if he counts the ignorant, the American people will appear
to be the most enlightened community in the world. The whole
population ... is situated between these two extremes."*

While I can't offer a substantive argument for the U.S. leading most of
Europe in literacy during that period of time or Tocqueville's observation of Americans "appearing to be the most enlightened" people in the
world, I would venture to speculate that it is in ways associated with
the freedom of opportunity afforded the American people in the new
Republic. The Founders established a federal government subordinate
to individual freedoms, placing power and authority in the natural ability of localized governments who have a better understanding of, and
are more effective and efficient in, meeting specific individual needs.
In other words, in the United Sates, the federal government yields authority to local government over such personal matters as education,
as opposed to top-down edicts from central or national governments,
such as was the case in the European aristocracies of their time. It could
also be associated with the transfer of the Protestant Reformation from
Europe to the New World, predominantly in the New England states,
since in these people the ability to read scripture was fundamental to the
practice of their faith. In support of this argument it turns out that within
the United States, literacy was also found in higher concentrations in
New England than in the South. The formation of local taxpayer-funded
schooling was also established and progressed earlier throughout New
England than in the Southern states and Europe. By the mid-1800s Massachusetts passed the first laws making school attendance compulsory
and began separating children into grades by age. By contrast, most
European countries lagged the U.S. in such milestones by more than
20 years. Well into the late 1800s the United States remained predom-

inately Protestant by a considerable majority. When large numbers of Catholics began immigrating to the U.S., many states began passing what were called Blaine Amendments, which forbade tax money from being used to fund parochial schools. This was directed at surges in predominantly Irish Catholic immigrants and intended to force their assimilation into American culture. Nevertheless, parochial schools (predominately Catholic) emerged and propagated in ethnic communities throughout the nation. It was not until the early 1900s that public school attendance became compulsory in all states, and secondary education, as we recognize it today, did not start to become commonplace until the mid-1900s. It is also worth noting that this evolution took place without the heavy hand of the federal government.

Similar to the early grade schools of America, most institutions of higher learning in early America were established by or were rooted in various religious denominations. Although established by the colonial legislature in Massachusetts, Harvard, which was the first college in colonial America, was initially focused on training young men for the ministry. William & Mary, which followed as the second college to be established in colonial America, was also established by the local legislature of Virginia, but it too had its roots in religion being closely associated with the Anglican Church. The early colleges that followed also had similar origins: Yale was founded by the Puritans, Princeton by the Presbyterians, Brown by the Baptists, and Columbia by the Anglicans, etc. These early colleges/universities were modeled after their English counterparts, such as Oxford and Cambridge, which were already well-established institutions of higher learning. In 1862 the Land Grant Act was passed, which provided land to the states expressly for the "endowment, support, and maintenance of at least one college where the leading object shall be, without excluding other scientific and classical studies and including military tactics, to teach such branches of learning as are related to agriculture and the mechanic arts, in order to promote the liberal and practical education of the industrial classes in the several pursuits and professions in life." In the early 1900s, there were fewer than 1,000 colleges, with about 160,000 students in the United States. By the year 2000 the number of colleges grew by more than five-fold, with over 1.5 million degrees awarded annually. Higher education in the U.S. has grown to become the envy of the world and is now the top destination for globally mobile students, annually hosting about one million students from other countries.

Today illiteracy globally is less than 10% for men and less than 20% for women; whereas, just two centuries prior these rates were more than 80%. As with many of the other demographic measures worldwide, these numbers vary proportionately similar to those for relative prosperity verses poverty.

OLD MAIN (PSU) – One of the first "land-grant" universities.

Within the preceding text I've made multiple references to observations documented by an impartial observer who came to America during the Jacksonian era. Alexus de Tocqueville, a French Aristocrat, came to America and traveled about the United States over a ten-month period in 1831 and 1832. Years later, back in France, he published what came to be a very famous work entitled *Democracy in America*. It was based upon his observations of the new Republic, as well as his interaction with a diversity of many Americans of the time, even calling upon then President Andrew Jackson. His writings, which I've drawn upon, provide an in depth study of many aspects of American democracy and American life in the early Republic, including the subjects of both religion and education in America, but I believe the following excerpt from his work provides as concise a summary as any, of both the nature and essence of the typical Americans he observed of the period.

> *"Everything about him is primitive and unformed, but he is himself the result of the labor and the experience of eighteen centuries. He wears the dress, and he speaks the language of cities; he is acquainted with the past, curious of the future, and ready for argument upon the present; he is, in short, a highly civilized being, who consents, for a time, to inhabit the backwoods, and who penetrates into the wilds of the New World with the Bible, an axe, and a file of newspapers."*

While I believe his words are intended to be very much a literal description of what he witnessed, the last few words double as metaphors for the three principle factors attributing to America's future prosperity: the Bible being representative of the moral compass provided by a Christian faith, the axe being representative of what came to be known as the Protestant work ethic, and the file of newspapers being representative of the general literacy of the populace.

Chapter 8

Transportation and Communications

"It was a beautiful day, the sun beat down, I had the radio on, I was drivin."

—Tom Petty

From the time that man first stood upright on his own two feet until the domestication of wild animals and the invention of the wheel, the only form of transportation available to him was that delivered by those same two feet. Similarly, from the time that man could first speak until maybe the harnessing of fire and the subsequent innovation of smoke signals, the greatest distance that he could communicate was as far as his voice would carry. We have come a long way since those times, with the ability to now travel halfway around the world in hours and to a nearby celestial body in a matter of days. We are now also able to communicate almost instantaneously, or more accurately at the speed of light, to points also halfway around the world, as well as the nearby cosmic bodies we have sent missions to. The history of the advancements that got us to this point is actually not all that long, if we don't dwell on the marginal advancements that took place over thousands of prehistoric years, such as those alluded to in the opening above.

Travel on horseback (as well as other alternative domesticated animals, such as the camel) or horse-drawn buggy or chariot served mankind well, for overland travel, for a considerably longer period than the combination of all the advancements in transportation that followed. This form of transportation dates back thousands of years, from before the Romans, the Greeks and even the Egyptians, and remained the principle form of long-distance travel well into the 1800s. Perhaps one of the final great migrations in which this form of travel was still in use was for the approximate 2,000-mile, six-month journey by wagon train from St. Louis, Missouri, to San Francisco, California, or other points west from the 1840s into the 1860s. This was an arduous and harrowing journey, in which an estimated 16,000 out of 400,000 pioneers who set out on the trip perished along the trail. The dangers were many and included disease, the most common of which was cholera, Indian attacks, exposure, drownings, attacks by wild animals, shootings, starvation, etc. One of the most noted and macabre tragedies of the era was the fate that befell the "Donner Party" when they became snowbound in the Sierra Nevada during the winter of 1846 to 1847. Of the 87 pilgrims who set out on their journey west, only 48 survived the ordeal, many of whom resorted to cannibalism to survive, eating the body parts of those who succumbed to starvation and other associated illnesses. But it was during the same period that the first commercially viable, mechanized form of transportation was being developed. Back east the first railroad in the United States, the Baltimore and Ohio (B&O), went into service in 1828. From that point on railroads spread rapidly throughout the United States, connecting most major commercial points east of the Mississippi by the start of the Civil War. Unfortunately for those earlier pioneers west of the Mississippi, the first transcontinental railroad did not go into service until 1869 during the Grant administration.

It was only seven years earlier, during the height of the Civil War, that President Abraham Lincoln had signed the Pacific Railroad Acts of 1862, making this milestone in American history possible. A journey that previously took months by horseback or wagon was now reduced to days. At the time the transcontinental railroad was completed there was a little more than 30,000 miles of track in the United States. By the end of the century that mileage had exploded to cover nearly 200,000 miles, reaching its peak of over 250,000 miles in 1916. At the beginning of the 1800s those traveling by stagecoach on the roads of the day, which would be difficult to classify as roads by most any modern standard, could make only about eight miles an hour on average, and that was with horses being changed out with well-rested ones about every 40 miles. In the first half of the century the early "rail ways," as they were referred to at the time, that began replacing this form of transportation were traveling at more than double that rate. Even in its early rudimentary form, with uneven tracks, trains were traveling at previously inconceivable speeds of 15 to 20 miles per hour. Later in the century, with further advances in locomotive technology and more importantly rail track construction, these speeds began to again double and even triple to the point that speeds in excess of 50 miles per hour were becoming common. Still travel in this century was lacking many of the creature comforts we have come to expect today. Wood- and later coal-fired steam engines would provide showers of ash and cinders for the passengers in the trailing cars. The lack of suspension in the undercarriage of passenger cars left passengers to endure uncomfortable and continual jostling on wooden seats, as well as the endless noise of the rattling and clanging cars, the driving engine, and the screeching of cast-iron wheels on steel rails. And let us not forget the lack of heat in the cold of winter and air conditioning in the heat of summer. Rail travel during this period was not necessarily safe either, although most modes of transportation weren't particularly safe in the 1800s. During that century, in any given decade there were typically 100 to more than 200 fatalities and thousands of injuries due to rail accidents. Although these numbers may not seem significant by today's standards, particularly when compared to automobile accident fatalities, they need to be considered in the context of the very small segment, of a much smaller population who had the opportunity to travel by rail during that period.

OCT. 22, 1895, TRAIN WRECK AT THE MONTPARNASSE TERMINAL, PARIS, FRANCE.

By the early 1900s, just as travel by rail was becoming more civilized with the production of much more comfortable, and sometimes lavish passenger cars being manufactured by the Pullman Car Company, mass production of the automobile was making another form of transportation available to the masses. Passenger rail travel reached its zenith during the first two decades of the 1900s and began to slowly decline thereafter. The advent of long-distance air travel and construction of the

Interstate Highway System after World War II both served to accelerate that decline. By the 1970s, passenger rail service in the United States was all but replaced by automobile and air travel when Amtrak was created to consolidate and take over the collapsing industry by the federal government.

At the start of the 1900s, the automotive manufacturing industry was in its infancy. The automobiles being produced were still open-air vehicles, which needed to be hand-cranked to start (no "automatic ignition" yet — i.e. key or push-button start) and were nearly void of anything that we today would consider creature comforts. Furthermore, there were no paved roads, except for in major cities or towns at that time. In summer, travel by automobile on dry days was hot, dusty, and dirty, bouncing over uneven rutted roads on vehicles that had very rudimentary suspension systems, not unlike those used on the horse-drawn carriages of the time. If it rained, you probably got very wet attempting to get your vehicle's canvas top in place, if you had one, but looking on the bright side, at least the rain would rinse away some of the dirt from your clothes when you needed to push it from being stuck in the mud. In the winter you would need to endure the cold as much as you would have in a horse-drawn carriage, except that the horse started much more easily in cold temperatures than the internal combustion engines of the period. On top of that, you needed to possess some mechanical abilities since breakdowns and flat tires were altogether common occurrences. It would be several years before many of the comforts and the anticipated reliability that we take for granted today would begin to become commonplace. The windshield wiper would not appear on automobiles until the late 1910s, and the intermittent wiper feature did not appear until another 50 years later. Fully enclosed automobiles with heating would arrive in the 1930s, and the AM radio arrived later that same decade.

Most of the other major developments came after World War II, when the Interstate Highway System came into being and automobile ownership became much more common for a majority of Americans. The automatic transmission and power steering became generally standard in most automobiles in the 1960s, and air conditioning followed in the 1970s. Safety equipment, such as seatbelts, became common in most cars of the 1960s and 1970s, and air bags and anti-lock brakes were introduced in the 1980s. The year 1983 saw one of the most seminal moments in automotive design with the introduction of the built-in cupholder by Chrysler when they introduced their new minivans. Within only a few years most new cars coming off the assembly lines of Detroit had cupholders, and by the end of the decade, they were as ubiquitous as any other feature auto shoppers expected to see in a new car. Since that time other features, such as stereo systems, zone climate controls, GPS, hands-free phone systems, all of which can now be voice activated and controlled, have come to be nearly as commonplace.

Air travel would follow a nearly parallel developmental period as that of the automobile, with the first successful flight being accredited to Wilbur and Orville Wright on December 17, 1903. That first recorded flight, which lasted only 12 seconds, took Orville 20 feet into the air and across 120 feet of a windswept beach in North Carolina. From there the Wright Brothers, as well as others, continued to develop the science of flight, but the most rapid advancements came as the result of World Wars I and II. Although Lindbergh made his historic solo transatlantic flight in 1927, it was not until the post-war period following World War II that commercial passenger air travel became fashionable, and then it was only for the wealthy. Air travel for the most part remained the domain of the wealthy and business travelers up through the start of the jet age in the 1960s. The transition from air propulsion by piston engine driven propellers to gas turbine jet engines in the 1960s and the introduction of "wide-body" designs in the 1970s significantly reduced operating costs and opened air travel to a broader segment of the general public. Deregulation of the airlines in the late 1970s and early 1980s further reduced ticket prices to the point where air travel became possible for average Americans. In fact, the ticket cost for an average American air traveler, based upon inflation adjusted dollars, is today almost half of what it was in 1980. The result is that about one billion U.S. passengers fly annually as opposed to about 250 million in 1980. A cross-continental trip that less than two centuries ago took six months, now takes less than six hours, with little thought given to the hazards involved. Moreover, modern day complaints about comfort and inconvenience are grossly overstated by comparison.

To this point I have focused solely on over land travel and have yet to address another form of transportation critical to the early development of mankind and still today essential to modern commerce. Travel by water was readily known of and used for ease of transport, as opposed to overland travel, well before any of the technological advances of the past two centuries. In fact, technological advances in nautical pursuits began and outpaced those for overland travel by centuries. However, its limitations are readily obvious, in that it is reliant upon the existence of navigable waterways to reach your intended destination. With this limitation readily evident, as well as the considerable advantages available to commerce through the ease of transporting large quantities of goods economically by water, it comes as little surprise that many of the earliest urban centers, based in trade, were founded and flourished along the world's great waterways and its oceans' natural harbors. Until the Industrial Revolution, travel by water was powered by the strength of the oarsmen, wind-driven sail, and natural currents through the millennia. From Columbus's first voyage in 1492 up through the early 1800s, transatlantic travel by sail took an average of six weeks. Pilgrims traveling west during the gold rush of the mid-1800s and opted not to take the overland route faced a stormy and dangerous 14,000-mile voyage of five to seven months around Cape Horn at the southern tip of South America. By 1900 with the advent of steam powered ships a transatlantic trip was reduced to less than a week, and in 1915 with the newly completed Panama Canal the voyage from New York City to San Francisco took less than four weeks. The transatlantic trip can be made today by air in less than six hours, and in even half that time up until the Concorde was taken out of service in 2003.

Transportation is, and has been, far more than just moving people from one point to another, and for the various modes throughout history this is the case for maritime shipping far more than the others. Regardless of all the technological advancements made in the past two centuries, shipping remains the most economical means of mass transport and international commerce. It has also been made necessary by the fact that nearly three quarters of the earth's surface is covered by water. For these reasons, today the vast majority of great urban centers remain coastal port cities. Over land, the rail systems came into being and had evolved through the Industrial Age to replace the canals of the late 1700s and early 1800s, becoming a very economical form of overland transport for a boundless array of vast quantities of commercial goods. To a much greater extent commercial maritime shipping has evolved from the days of sail to move ever increasing volumes and tonnage in a fraction of the time. Although data on the tonnage of international trade in the early 1800s is varied, it could be measured in the tens of millions of tons, whereas today it can be measured in the billions of tons. The carrying capacity of merchant ships has also increased in just as mind boggling of proportions. The cargo capacity of an average early 1800s merchant ship of sail was measured in the hundreds of tons, whereas today most merchant ships carry cargos ranging from 20,000 to 400,000 tons. Other than localized ferry services, the cruise industry is probably the last remnant of passenger service that remains with us today, and it does not just remain, but it thrives. In the 1960s it had appeared that the emergence of jet air travel would be fatal to the great ocean liners of decades past. As airlines began cutting into transatlantic ocean liner service, marketing in the industry shifted focus from transportation toward leisure and/ or vacation cruising. Focus also began shifting from exclusive luxury service for the wealthy elite to a much broader and growing market of middle-class vacationers when the *Queen Elizabeth II* (QE-2) inaugurated "one-class cruising," in which all passengers received the same quality berthing, facilities, and amenities. The vacation cruise industry got a further boost in the 1970s when it was popularized by the hit TV series *Love Boat.* Since that time, the number of cruising passengers has more than doubled every ten years to currently exceed 25 million passengers annually.

Of the 25 million annual cruise passengers, nearly 15 million come from the United States. This means that out of a population of little more than 300 million, nearly 5% of the U.S. population has the leisure time and excess funds available to float about the world's seas with little else to do other than indulge in excesses of food, drink, and sun. Vacationing of course is not just limited cruising, as it is estimated that approximately half of all Americans vacation annually, spending an estimated $100 billion on those vacations. Contemplating a vacation may seem to be just another norm in our modern lives, but in the relatively recent past, Americans' dreams of the vast number of experiences available to them often exceed their ability to attain them. But the ability to dream these

dreams and enjoy the vacations we are able to attain has evolved to become real and commonplace only during the latter half of the last century. Until that time the transportation required to facilitate such dreams
and make them real was beyond the means of the common man, and
leisure pursuits, such as a vacation, were only possible for those of considerable means.

Other than the spoken word, communication via the written word has
been with mankind for some 5,000 years, evolving from etchings on
stone to clay tablets, then onto papyrus and animal skins until paper
was invented by the Chinese in about 100 BC. Although paper did reach
Europe from the Far East via trade, it was not until about 1250 AD that
it started to be produced in Italy; from there, it was then sold throughout
Europe. The next major advancement was the printing press that was
invented by a German named Johann Gutenberg in the 1430s. Gutenberg used his press and paper to reproduce copies of the Bible. Limited
reproduction of the written word was less about limitations in the technology of the time and due more to the reality that most people could
not read. Therefore, most printed materials remained the purview of the
church during this period in European history. For similar reasons, early
European postal services were generally the dominion of religious entities, connecting abbeys, monasteries, and churches, which were oases
of literacy in Europe during the 1400s through the 1700s.

In the early American colonies, literacy significantly outpaced most of
the world's population and reliable communication between the colonies
was considered vital to the cause of liberty. In 1775 the Second Continental Congress appointed Benjamin Franklin to be the first Postmaster

General of the rebelling colonies. Later, after the war, the United States Postal Service was formally established as part of the nation's founding. Communication by post was considered so fundamental and so critical to the new Republic that the founders, under Article 1, Section 8 of the U.S. Constitution, made it an institution of the federal government. The Constitution also specifically required the establishment of "post roads" since most roads of the period were used as much for communication, if not more than for travel. Much of the early mail was transported by boat and then by steamboat starting in 1815 since waterways provided greater and faster access to many communities than overland routes, if an overland route even existed. The time it took for news, a letter, or other communication to get from one place to another was still purely a function of the speed of transport, varying from days to weeks within the eastern states and even months with European nations. The last major battle, and possibly the most noted of the War of 1812, was the Battle of New Orleans, which was fought on January 8, 1815. In this conflict Andrew Jackson's defending forces defeated a superior British force that outnumbered his own by nearly two to one. During the incursion, Jackson's forces suffered approximately 300 casualties to the British losses of nearly 25 hundred. Two weeks earlier, back in Europe, the Treaty of Ghent was signed on December 24, 1814, ending the war two weeks before Jackson's rout of the British at New Orleans, but it took more than a month before news of the treaty reached America. Since news of Jackson's resounding victory spread throughout the states well in advance of the news from Ghent, to many it had appeared that Jackson's victory was responsible for ending the war.

Through most of the early 1800s, the speed of communications advanced only as fast as the innovations in transportation. People living on the West Coast, in California's major cities, such as San Francisco, lived in a kind of time warp, with information of events on the East Coast and from Europe taking several months to reach them, and responses taking months more to return. In the early 1800s the Pony Express reduced the transport of correspondence between the two coasts to under two weeks. The Pony Express was a private enterprise, which despite its successes in speed of transport, never became financially viable, and in spite being somewhat romanticized retrospectively, it lasted only 18 months. It was not until after the Civil War and completion of the Transcontinental Railroad that mail service between the coasts could be measured in days. But while the railroads were becoming the primary mode of transport for mail and parcels by the Postal Service, their dominance in speed of communication was also short lived. In 1844 Samuel Morse sent his first message via telegraph from Washington, DC, to Baltimore, Maryland. In 1861 Western Union had laid the first transcontinental telegraph line, and in 1866 the first transatlantic line had been laid, making communications around the world near instantaneous from that point forward.

THE OVERLAND-PONY EXPRESS.—[PHOTOGRAPHED BY SAVAGE, SALT LAKE CITY, FROM A PAINTING BY GEORGE M. OTTINGER.]

AN ARTIST REPRESENTATION OF THE PONY EXPRESS BEING REPLACED BY THE TELEGRAPH.

Although the ultimate limiting speed of communication, at least based upon physics as we know today, had been reached in the mid 1800s, the advancement of communications continued in the many platforms and uses that followed. Although earlier inventers are credited with developing various forms of the telephone, Alexander Graham Bell was awarded its first patent in 1876. His work was based upon earlier work in electromagnetics by names such as Hertz, Maxwell, and Tesla. Guglielmo Marconi is generally credited with inventing the radio in the 1890s. Subsequently, on Christmas Eve, 1906, the first public radio broadcast was made by Canadian inventor Reginald Fessenden. Later the television was developed by a multitude of contributors in the early 1900s. All of these inventions found their way into the homes of average Americans in the early to mid-1900s. The first was the radio in the 1930s, followed by the telephone in the 1940s, and TVs in the 1950s. All these technologies continued in development through the 1900s and into the 2000s. Vacuum tubes were replaced by transistors, reducing costs and energy requirements, as well as allowing for much more compact componentry. Landlines gave way to cellular and satellite transmission; black-and-white TV became color TV, as well as ever-increasing audio and visual quality and reliability. With each of these technological advancements also came advancements in production and the economy of scale. As these technologies evolved, our capitalistic free enterprise system continually drove down prices, making each successive stride forward available to much broader and more diverse segments of the population.

In the 1990s another completely new technological development came about that revolutionized the world we live in today. The origin of the internet may be a point of dispute, but one thing is fairly certain: contrary to an urban myth the internet was not invented by Al Gore. Regardless of its origin, it not just revolutionized communication, but it has found its way into countless aspects of our daily lives: education, entertainment, manufacturing, and transportation to name just a few general categories, for which there are many more subcategories. In conjunction with the advent of personal computing, the internet can be used to assist us in solving here-to-for impossibly difficult and complex mathematical and scientific problems, or we can use it to order next day home delivery of our pets' meds. Although not in and of itself a form of communication, the development of the computer in the later portion of the last century and into the 2000s has revolutionized modern life. The iPhone or Android phone you hold in your hand has at least a thousand times the computing power of the Apollo 11 Guidance Computer that landed the first "man on the moon and brought him safely back to earth" in 1969. And what does all that computing power add to the daily lives of the average American? Well for starters, there's Facebook, Instagram and Twitter, as well as a nearly limitless number of video games. And besides the ability to text and send e-mail, you can even make a phone call with it! It is estimated that approximately eight hours of the average American's day is spent texting, browsing the web, playing video games, or simply watching TV. What on God's good earth could we have done with all that time in days past?

Chapter 9

Food, Water, and Shelter

"There are people in the world so hungry, that God cannot appear to them except in the form of bread."

—Mahatma Gandhi

In the opening chapter we addressed many issues under the heading of "The Necessities of Life," the majority of which are little more than what we may perceive as necessary to make humanity tolerable in our modern world. Other than the air we breathe, which requires no real effort to satisfy our need for it, food, water, and shelter are indeed the generally recognized bare essentials necessary for man to survive. Survivalists categorize the importance of each of these to sustain life with what is called the "Rule of Threes." You can generally only live for approximately three minutes without air, three hours without shelter (in adverse weather conditions), three days without water, and three weeks without food. Early in life, from the time of our birth, we are dependent upon others to provide our food, water, and shelter to ensure our survival until we attain an age where we can fend for ourselves, and then we in turn care for our offspring, perpetuating the cycle through the generations. This cycle has continued, with minimal change, throughout the history of human existence on this planet.

The industrial and technological advances and changes to the human condition that have occurred over the past two hundred years are an exponential aberration when compared to the sum total of all that came before. It is no stretch to state that for easily more than 99.9% of man's existence, our near-total focus, preoccupation, and efforts were toward satisfying our needs for food, water, and shelter. Today, for most of the developed world, all three are readily available in abundance with little to no effort and are nearly taken for granted. Recent advances in the ready availability of potable water have already been addressed in several of the preceding chapters. The following paragraphs will therefore focus on food and shelter.

Today, when it comes to food, we find ourselves mostly preoccupied in the decision-making process about what we want to eat as opposed to any other aspect of the food that we do eat. In fact, most people today are focused more on eating less, rather than eating enough. In the United States and most of the developed world, food is readily available in what would appear to be limitless abundance and variety, making our consumption of it more a function of appetite than hunger. Little more than a century ago the vast variety and quantities of affordable food available in a typical grocery store of today would have been as unimaginable as air travel, the television, or the mobile phone.

As far back as 20,000 BC mankind was collecting various wild grains to support its diet. Between 5,000 BC and 10,000 BC, mankind began cultivating many of the grains we are familiar with today, such as wheat, barley, and rice. Around 10,000 BC mankind also began domesticating animals, such as pigs, goats, sheep, and, later, cattle. Over the 10,000 years that followed the varieties of plants and animals coming under its dominion increased, as did the methods of planting, growing, and cultivating crops and breeding, raising, and slaughtering livestock. However, change came slowly, in fact so very slowly it would appear negligible from generation to generation, and it was certainly impossible to detect in any single lifetime. More important than any single or series of marginal developments was man's long-term influence upon the crops and animals he had a hand in propagating. Over the majority of those millennia man, through his unintentional but fortuitous intervention, was engaging in a form of genetic engineering through the selective cultivation and breeding of his crops and livestock. Man chose to propagate those plants and animals with traits most beneficial to him over those he considered less desirable. The result was more durable produce bearing more bountiful seeds of grain and edible fruit and livestock with better and better temperament for domestication, as well as larger and heartier breeds. It is not clear when, but at some point, mankind became aware of its influence, and its efforts became intentional, further enhancing the process. Today we enjoy the benefit of many grains, fruits, vegetables, and domesticated animals (including our pet dogs and cats) that bear only a marginal resemblance to their ancient ancestors, and without man's continued intervention they would have difficulty surviving and propagating on their own in the wild.

By the time the early colonies of North America were established and became self-sustaining there were a handful of farming innovations accrued over the millennia that were vital to produce yields beyond the individual farmer's basic needs. The most obligatory of which include:

❖ The plow that was drawn by domesticated beasts of burden, typically a horse or oxen.

❖ Crop rotation and leaving alternate fields fallow each season, promoting recovery of the soil for future planting.

❖ Fertilization of the soil using manure from their domesticated livestock.

By the time of the American Revolution these basics, which were as fundamental to farming then as they are today, were reasonably well-understood and practiced. The excess yields they provided freed mankind to contemplate and act upon other pursuits beyond their mere existence and daily survival. At this time in history the United States was still predominately an agrarian society with many of the best-known founders such as Washington, Jefferson, and Adams known in their time for their principle vocation as planters or farmers. The surplus yields of their plantations and farms, in conjunction with those provided by the masses of lesser-known farmers, made it possible for others, such as John Hancock to pursue his livelihood as a merchant and Alexander Hamilton to pursue professions in the law and banking. More important to all of us today was the time freed up to facilitate their collective efforts in the founding of the United States of America. The extensive writings by the planting/farming segment of these founders consumed as many pages recording weather, crop rotation, manure preparation, and application as they did of theory and discourse on democracy. But even with the advances of that time and the advancement of farming as a science being studied, starvation and famine remained a widespread and all too common circumstance of life for many. It is difficult today to read any literature written of the Revolutionary War period that eludes mention of the starvation and malnutrition that Washington's armies endured, not just at Valley Forge, but through every winter of that campaign. Although farming had evolved to generate surpluses for alternate pursuits, it was still largely inadequate to sustain armies in the field for extended periods. Further compounding the difficulty of feeding an army was the inability to preserve what excess stores of food were available from an annual harvest. Certainly, they were without modern refrigeration, but the innovation of a technique for preserving perishable goods by canning or jarring had yet to be devised.

Not unlike many great innovations through history, war would become the mother of invention for a means to preserve the food to feed armies and subsequently the masses. In the early 1800s Napoleon through successive campaigns continued to face the difficulty of feeding large armies in the field, much as his predecessors had. Subsequently, he offered an award of 12,000 francs to whoever could develop a reliable way to preserve food to sustain his armies and in turn his desire for conquest. In 1810 another Frenchman by the name of Nicolas Appert claimed the prize when he perfected a technique he had already been working on to preserve food through a process of heating (and unbeknownst to him sterilizing) the food and sealing it in jars. Later, in 1812, an Englishman by the name of Brian Donkin took the process one step further by sealing the sterilized food in unbreakable tin cans in lieu of using glass containers. The innovation of preserving foods by jarring and canning was not just a major milestone in military history, but it was also a breakthrough for sustaining crews at sea. However, as much a breakthrough as it indeed was, there was a negative consequence that the people of the early 1800s were totally unaware of. Not only did they not fully understand the process of killing bacteria through the heating of food prior to sealing it in containers, they also didn't understand, or more accurately were unaware of, the hazards of using lead solder to seal the cans.

In 1845 a British expedition of 129 men, led by John Franklin, set sail aboard the HMS *Erebus* and the HMS *Terror* to find a Northwest Passage around the American continent to the Far East. After remaining unheard from for three years, the first of several successive search expeditions was launched to find what became of Franklin's party. Franklin and his crew remained lost until 1850 when the first relics of his original expedition were found. Later expeditions found evidence of cannibalism amongst the remains of the crew that were found and exhumed. It was not until the 1980s that scientists studying those remains postulated that the crew may have succumbed to madness brought upon by lead poisoning from the ships' stores that were sealed in tin cans with lead solder.

Up until the discovery of jarring and canning foods for preservation there were few alternatives other than sun drying or other forms of dehydration, such as smoking, brining and/or packing in salt, pickling with acids such as vinegar, or fermentation and distilling foods into drinkable spirits. All of these are still with us today, but more as a form of preparing foods for our consumption based upon a desired taste and rarely as a means of preservation without refrigeration. They did however remain common forms of preservation in conjunction with the growth of canning and jarring well into the early 1900s. Although the icebox was introduced in the early 1800s, it did not become common in average American households until near the end of that century. The icebox remained a primary form of preserving food in the household in the early 1900s until it was slowly replaced by the electric refrigerator between the 1930s and 1950s. As difficult as it may be for us today to believe or understand, up through the 1800s people still consumed rancid and molding foods on all too regular a basis. The fact that rancid food may smell and/or taste bad, even very bad, does not necessarily mean it is unsafe for consumption. Now, this is where we need to be careful, very careful. For most modern Americans any consideration of eating rancid or molding foods is hardly conceivable. However, for most modern-day

Americans real hunger is just as difficult to conceive. Regardless, the smell of rancid food is a good indicator that it may not be safe to eat. This is not because of the oxidation of fat compounds that cause the bad smell and tastes associated with rancid foods; it is because the smell is an indicator that deadly bacteria may also be present.

Up through the Civil War it was still very common to pack meats in barrels of salt to preserve it (i.e. salt pork) for very long periods. This method of preservation was done not to keep it from becoming rancid, which it didn't, but to keep the deadly bacteria out. And this was at a time when there was still no understanding of bacteria. The knowledge of preserving meats with salt came, like most all other methods of preservation, through years of trial and error; — by determining what was lethal, or not, in times of deprivation and/or desperation. The practice of meat preservation by packing it in barrels of salt was very common for hundreds, if not thousands, of years on long voyages at sea. Try to stretch your mind and your senses to comprehend as near reasonably as possible what it may have been like to eat boiled pork that had been stored in a barrel of salt on the decks or down in the bowels of your wooden ship, for months on end at sea. Worse even, in the heat of the Caribbean or South Pacific tropics.

During the Civil War, the standard daily ration that a typical Union foot soldier subsisted on included 20 oz. of salt pork or salt beef, 12 oz. of hard bread (referred to as "hardtack"), and 1 oz. of desiccated mixed vegetables. The hardtack was a very dense and hard dried biscuit or cracker. It was often infested with worms, likely flour moth larvae and/ or rice weevils that were left floating in the soldier's coffee after he would dip the hardtack in it to soften it, thereby making it easier to consume. Since food was often in low supply, the average Union soldier was nevertheless generally grateful for what he did receive, which was consistently better than that of his Confederate counterpart. It was an altogether common perception by the average Civil War soldier that the maggots and weevils were better fed than they were.

By the time of the Civil War, agricultural output per acre of farmland had already increased severalfold from that of the Middle Ages. If not for the basic advancements accrued to that point it would have been impossible, even with the meager rations the troops did receive, to maintain the large armies of the North or South in the field for any extended period, let alone the four years that the conflict lasted. But the really big changes were yet to come. In the mid-1800s more than half of all Americans were still engaged in farming for their livelihood. By the end of the 1900s, it was less than 2%. The mid-1800s into the early 1900s were a transitional period for farming, with increases in farm production and decreases in acreage placed into production to keep pace with the population growth over the same period. Then in the 1930s production began to explode, based in part on the following technological achievements/milestones:

- ❖ In the first decade of the 1900s the use of commercial fertilizers doubled since the introduction of the product in the late 1800s; by the 1930s it doubled again.

- ❖ During the first decade of the 1900s, the first farm tractors powered by an internal combustion engine went into commercial production. Less than a century earlier, in 1837, a blacksmith in Illinois was innovating plow design. His name: John Deere. Later the company that bears his name will introduce the John Deere the Model "A" tractor during the Great depression in 1934, establishing a benchmark for durability and reliability in the farm tractor industry.

A 1930S JOHN DEERE FARM TRACTOR – The early dependability and reliability of its tractors made the name "John Deere" almost synonymous with the farm tractor. *Image provided as Courtesy of John Deere.*

❖ In 1905 the first agricultural engineering curriculum was introduced at Iowa State College. Other universities across the United States follow in rapid succession with similar courses of study.

❖ During the second decade of the 1900s, the American Harvester Company went into commercial production with the first mechanized harvesting equipment although it was still powered by horses.

❖ In the 1920s the International Harvester Company introduced the "power take-off" on its tractors. This feature provided for the transfer of power from the tractor to the harvesting equipment that was attached to it. Subsequently, unemployment for farm draft horses increased dramatically.

❖ The 1920s also saw the first aerial dusting of crops in the field with pesticides and herbicides.

❖ In the early 1930s the first baling machines were introduced, which, when attach to a farm tractor, pick up cut hay in the field and then shape and compress it into a 16x18-inch bale. Later that same decade, a self-tying feature was added, which ties the bales with twine.

❖ In the late 1930s the first self-propelled combines are introduced. As its name implies, this equipment combines two farming operations (threshing and reaping) into a single machine.

THE INTERNATIONAL HARVESTER COMBINE – First-of-its-kind innovation also made the name "International Harvester" nearly synonymous with farm equipment. *Image provided Courtesy of the Wisconsin Historical Society, WHS-78552.*

After the 1930s production began to explode, independent of the acreage of land put into farming. In the 1850s about 75 to 99 man-hours were required to produce 100 bushels of corn from about 2 ½ acres of land. By the 1930s, the labor required dropped to about 15 to 20 man-hours to produce the same yield from the same acreage. By the end of the 1900s, it only required 2 to 3 man-hours to produce the same yield, but now with less than half the acreage. In the 1930s one farmer could feed about ten people; by the end of the century, that same farmer could feed more than 100 people. The quantum leap in yields that took place in the latter half of the 1900s was less about industrialization and more about the science of agriculture. At first this was due primarily to advancements in fertilization, irrigation, care, and use of the land, and continued selective breading of crops and livestock; later these advancements began to include growing work on a microscopic level with Genetically Modified Organisms (GMOs). In conjunction with other industrial and scientific advancements of the last century, such as those achieved in refrigeration and transportation, we have come to enjoy exhaustive options in choices of food type and exhaustive options in choices of food source/preparation, as well as a very high quality of the foods we eat.

If you're reading these pages, it's a reasonably safe assumption that shelter is not one of your daily concerns. What's more, you are likely to be kicking back in your easy chair, in the comfort of a reasonable, well-appointed home or apartment. Unfortunately, even with all the achievements of the past century, particularly in the United States, homelessness is still with us. There is currently a homeless population in the United States estimated to be a little more than half a million, and in very recent years that number has been on the rise. This recent increase is in contradiction to the longer range trend since 2007, which was the first year that the Department of Housing and Urban Development (HUD) started collecting and publishing such data. Prior to that year estimates on the number of homeless are more or less conjecture and highly unreliable. What reliable information we do have comes from the 1930s and the Great Depression. During this time, it is estimated that there were two million homeless; keep in mind this was at a time when the U.S population was a little more than a third of what it is today. Although the period of the Great Depression was clearly representative of a spike in homelessness and an aberration from the norm, looking earlier into the 1800s, even without reliable data, it's a reasonable assumption that a significant segment of the population was homeless, as evidenced by certain literature of the period. Maybe an indirect indicator of how much improved this condition is today is the increased interest and concern that has gained focus in more recent years. It was not until the 1870s when the term "homelessness" was first used indicating that until then it was fairly common and not even recognized or acknowledged as an issue. Even well into the 1900s the homeless were on the margins of society, generally discounted and referred to as "tramps" or "hobos." There was a stigma attached to this segment of the population being transient vagrants, traversing the country in search of work and living off the handouts of others. More than anything else, the thriving economics of the Industrial Revolution gave many, if not most, of these people work, taking them off the streets and putting them into affordable housing.

THE LOG CABIN, which is a symbol of the American homestead on the frontier where lumber was readily available; in this case it's an old photo of Lincoln's Birthplace in Kentucky.

For the United States, as for much of the developed world, up to the 1800s much of the housing for the common man was provided from what he could assemble through his own toil and from the resources at hand, providing the most basic of shelter from the elements — much as it is still today for many of those throughout the undeveloped world. Even as time advanced well into the 1800s, homes on the frontier were still being constructed of adobe in the southwest and of sod on the prairies of the Midwest. Forested areas from the Appalachian Mountains to the Mississippi and in the Pacific Northwest were the domains of the log cabin. It was only in, or in close proximity to, more urban areas, the cities and villages of the day, where homes constructed of cut and milled lumber and masonry were to be found. The considerable majority of which were constructed of wood, which made the hazard of fire an ever-present danger to life and property. One of the earliest catastrophic fires in the history of New York City started on September 20th, 1776, and burned through the night into the 21st. There is still debate as to whether the fire was started by the revolutionaries fleeing the city, the British occupying the city, or if it was an inadvertent result of the battle that preceded these events. When the flames were finally doused, approximately 500 structures were destroyed, which was about a third of the city. Today we have generally lost sight of how extremely devastating and deadly urban fires were through the 1800s and into the 1900s. The following is a summary of just a few of the more notable to refresh your memory:

- ❖ 1814 — Washington, DC, was set ablaze by the British during the War of 1812, burning both the White House and Capitol Building, as well as other prominent structures. Fortunately, much of the city was saved by a severe storm, possibly a hurricane that hit the city the following day, putting out the fires. This was also the event from which Dolly Madison saved the famous Gilbert Stuart portrait of George Washington from the flames.

- ❖ 1835 — The Second Great Fire of New York City consumed approximately 17 city blocks, destroying hundreds of buildings and killing two people.

- ❖ 1849 — St. Louis is the victim of the worst fire in its history. The fire, which lasted eleven hours, destroyed an estimated 430 buildings, a significant portion of the city at that time. It also destroys 23 steamboats and other boats along the riverfront and killed three people, one of which was a firefighter who is believed to be the first firefighter to be killed in the line of duty.

- ❖ 1851 — San Francisco was a boomtown in the height of the gold rush when this fire destroyed nearly three quarters of the city, burning some 2,000 buildings and killing at least nine people. The fire was so intense that it was reportedly visible miles out at sea.

❖ 1861 through 1865 — During the American Civil War many southern cities were burned to the ground, including Atlanta, Georgia; Columbia, South Carolina; and Richmond, Virginia.

❖ 1871 — The Great Chicago fire is probably the best-known fire of the era. This is partly due to its severity, but also for the story of its being set by Mrs. O'Leary's cow knocking over a lantern, which is more likely based in myth than fact. The fire, which lasted three days, destroyed a little more than three square miles of downtown Chicago, killing approximately 300 people and leaving more than 100,000 homeless.

❖ 1906 — The Great San Francisco Earthquake and Fire is nearly as well known today as the 1871 Chicago fire. The fire was started by a magnitude 7.9 earthquake, which in and of itself was devastating, but what remained from the earthquake was consumed by the fire that followed. The fire, which was in reality multiple fires breaking out over a period of several days, destroyed about 80% of the city. Estimates of the dead reach as high as 3,000, but it is impossible to differentiate what portion is directly attributable to the earthquake and what portion to the fire.

Bucket brigades were still used to fight these types of urban fires in America up until the mid-1800s when the first Fire Companies were established. Hand-pump fire engines, which were generally pulled by the firefighters to the fires, were still in use into the 1850s when the first steam powered fire-pump engines were introduced. As the engines got larger and heavier, particularly the steam powered fire-pump engines, the power to draw them shifted from manpower to horsepower.

The horse-drawn, steam-powered fire-pump engine continued in use for fighting fires through the second half of the 1800s and into the early 1900s when both the steam engine and horses were replaced by the internal combustion engine. Much of the early construction in major East Coast cities, such as New York, prior to the 1800s made use of readily available timber as the primary building material. As these cities grew to be more densely populated, with closely packed wooden structures, the hazard of devastating and deadly fires grew in parallel. The tragedies of the many epic fires of the 1800s was a principle driving force in transitioning these urban areas from wood to masonry during the same period. Fires during this period were not just deadly, but also typically a devastating total financial loss for the proprietor and/or homeowner. Up until the 1800s the insurance business, which had already been in existence for over a century, was principally engaged in maritime underwriting. Benjamin Franklin was instrumental in kick-starting the fire insurance business in the Americas, but it would not be until the late 1800s that it would become reliable enough to be in widespread use.

At the beginning of the 1900s the typical American home was about 700 to 1,200 square feet, with two to three bedrooms and maybe a bathroom, or just as likely maybe not. About 20% of the population, typically in the more urban areas, lived in crowded one or two room units, housing entire multi-generational families. Much of this housing still lacked basic amenities, such as plumbing and central heat. From 1900 to the 1950s home ownership remained nearly flat at around 45%, but that number jumped to more than 60% during the post-war 1950s. However, the nature of the housing did not change that much. Although home ownership jumped dramatically during the decade of the 1950s, the homes still had just 1,000 square feet of living space on average and still had just two bedrooms, although the bathroom became a common amenity along with plumbing, central heat, and even electricity in nearly three quarters of American households. Mail order homes from Sears, Roebuck and Co., which made home ownership viable for some rural Americans in decades past, were giving way to suburban developments, such as Levittown in New York. Many of these homes still housed several generations of the same family.

Through the fifty years that followed there was little variation in the percentage of home ownership, but by the end of the century the nature of the housing Americans were becoming accustomed to had changed dramatically. At the start of the 2000s the average size of a typical new home had more than doubled to over 2,000 square feet, with standard layouts including three bedrooms and two and a half baths. In the '60s and '70s central air was becoming an option in new homes, and most were being built with a one-car garage, which was generally standard. By the '80s and '90s new homes came standard with central air conditioning and at least a two-car garage. In just fifty years the landscape of America was transformed from suburban family farms to suburban residential developments. Even with the size of housing doubling over this period, and the addition of all those amenities, housing prices remained relatively flat. According to the National Association of Home Builders (NAHB), while median household incomes rose from approximately $3,300 in 1950 to $45,000 in 2000, the average cost of new housing grew from $11,000 to $195,000 over the same period. That means that the average home in the 1950s cost about 3.3 times the median income; in 2000 it had increased to 4.3 times the median income. Since the square footage of housing on average roughly doubled over the same period, on a square foot basis the cost actually came down. The problem became that we just had a lot more to spend our money on. This included the cost of electricity for our A/C, phone, cable, and internet service, and, of course, the cars in the garage, as well as all that other stuff in the garage — the lawn mower, hedge trimmer, snow blower, etc.

Of course, things definitely went sideways in the 2000s with the housing crisis and subsequent recession, but then this event could be, and has been the subject of many other books. In short it has become convenient to just blame the "fat cat Wall Street bankers." But if we're going to be honest, we all had a hand in it. From the average home buyer trying to keep up with the Joneses and signing up for mortgages they knew or should have known they couldn't afford to all those realtors, mortgage brokers, and bankers, selling mortgages to people who could not substantiate they had adequate financial resources, but had a pulse and could sign their name to an appraisal industry that only saw the appreciation of real estate through rose-colored glasses to the average Joes that saw the same and overnight joined the many speculators, flipping houses in their spare time. And finally, at the top of the pyramid, the politicians so eager to promote the "irrational exuberance," riding the wave of their own narcissistic self-promotion. In the end it's just easier, and feels better, to blame the other guy, and the fat cat Wall Street bankers are an easy and favorite target.

This evening you may be sitting in your home, in the comfort of your easy chair and climate-controlled living space (A/C in summer and heating in winter) enjoying some entertainment, music on your stereo, watching television, or simply reading by the light provided from electricity. As it nears dinner time your appetite builds, and let's now suppose you have the desire to eat a cheeseburger. Even if you don't particularly care for a cheeseburger please bear with me as it's just an example, and anyway, I just so happen to like cheeseburgers. Moreover, it's a good example because the cheeseburger includes elements from each of the four food groups. So, take for example the cheeseburger, one of the most ubiquitous foods in modern day America. In fact, Americans eat an estimated 50 billion burgers annually. That translates to about three burgers a week for the average American, who also has a nearly limitless number of options to choose from.

For starters there are of course the big-name fast food chains, such as McDonald's, Burger King, and Wendy's, to choose from. Or you could go a bit more upscale or "gourmet" with Five Guys or Red Robin, or if you live in the Southwest United States, you may well go for an In-N-Out burger. You could even choose from any one of the tens of thousands of independent local burger joints spread all across America; in fact, you'd be hard pressed to walk into any restaurant, other than maybe specialty ethnic restaurants (pizzerias, Chinese, Mexican, sushi, etc.), that don't have burgers on their menu. If you choose not to leave the comfort of your home and have the time and inclination, you may want to cook your own burger. You could cook it on a charcoal grill, but if that's too much trouble, you could use your gas grill. Or you could just cook it indoors on your stove top or even broil it in your gas or electric oven. You could even microwave your burger, but wait, who microwaves a burger anyway? Too many choices to contemplate, and who needs the stress anyway? So in the final analysis you opt to pick up your mobile phone and call in an order for a "California cheeseburger," a side of fries, and Coke to be delivered to your front door. Ever contemplate how different this simple act may have been 50, 100, or even 150 years ago?

50 Years Ago (1970): The major fast food burger joints we are accustomed to today are in their infancy. McDonald's has only about 1,000 restaurants nationally. Burger King had little more than 250, and Wendy's has just one in Columbus, Ohio. Most of the others didn't exist yet, and certainly there were none of the upscale or "gourmet" restaurants, such as Five Guys or Red Robin, which came along much later. So, unless you lived in Columbus, Ohio, or another urban area where one of the others may have existed, you were out of luck with respect to this option. You did still have the option of going to a neighborhood restaurant where you had a high probability of getting a pretty good burger. And you could always make it at home where you had many of the options available as you do today, except that if you are one of those few who would cook a burger in a microwave, there is the very high probability that you didn't have one. Just one other thought. If its summertime, you may want to opt for having a cook-out on your grill since you most likely didn't have A/C yet either.

100 Years Ago (1920): There are no fast food burger joints. The first of its kind, White Castle, would not be opened until a year later, on September 13, 1921, in Wichita, Kansas. When it comes to your neighborhood restaurants, it's doubtful that you would find any burgers on any menu either. Just fourteen years earlier Upton Sinclair had published his book *The Jungle*, revealing the unsanitary practices that were prevalent in the meat packing industry. Although the book had a widespread positive impact on reforming the industry, it led to a general distrust of ground beef amongst most of the public that would last for decades to come. You could of course endeavor to make one at home, but first you would need to start a wood or coal fire in your stove. You may have procured the ground beef earlier from your local butcher, but if not, you could always grind the beef at home in your counter-top, hand-crank meat-grinder. The rolls were readily available from your local baker, but, like many, you would probably bake them at home. Even the cheese and tomato ketchup should be readily available from your local general store, but other garnishes like lettuce, tomato, or onion would only be available if in season. At least you could listen to the radio while you ate.

150 Years Ago (1870): The American hamburger or cheeseburger did not exist, or at least any semblance of what we today recognize it to be. Although some trace its origins back to Hamburg, Germany, or the Earl of Sandwich, the American hamburger's genesis came about by any one or a combination of people claiming to be its founder in the period from the 1880s through to the early 1900s. So, if in 1870 you were to have invented the cheeseburger in advance of any of its other possible founders, you would have had to do it at home. If you were an average American at the time, you would have probably lived on your family's farm, providing you with most every resource you would need. You would, however, need to plan ahead, very much ahead, raising a cow to slaughter and butcher, but if it's your only cow, you'd want to milk it first, so you could make the cheese. You would need to grow the wheat and grind it into flower to bake the rolls, and you would have to plan to do all this in the fall when the lettuce, tomato, and onions would also be available fresh from your garden for harvest. Ketchup may present a bit of a problem, since Mr. Heinz would not launch commercial production of the condiment for another six years, but you may be able to concoct some facsimile from one of the recipes available at the time. The making of your French fries should not present an issue since their origin dates back to late 1700s Paris, France, although without ketchup, you may want to eat them with mayonnaise much as the French do today. This condiment has also been around since the late 1700s, also having its origins in France. You will need to forgo your Coca-Cola since this soft drink will not be invented for another 16 years, by a pharmacist in Atlanta, Georgia. When you finally sit down to enjoy this culinary delight, the only entertainment may be the beauty of a natural sunset and the thought of later reading a book by candlelight.

So, this evening, when you sit back in that easy chair of yours to enjoy your home-delivered cheeseburger, instead of watching *The Bachelorette*, go to your stereo, dust off that old Jimmy Buffet album, and listen to "Cheeseburger in Paradise." That famous title phrase should now have a whole new meaning.

CHEESEBURGER IN PARADISE – You don't need to be in a tropical paradise to enjoy the simplicity and delectability of this culinary delight.

Chapter 10

A Day in the Life of the "Coal Man"

"Early to bed, early to rise, makes a man healthy, wealthy, and wise."

—*Benjamin Franklin*

It is 4:00 a.m. on a Friday morning as the Coal Man rises from his sleep. Without the aid of an alarm this routine is automatic, and although he has not slept well in recent days, he proceeds as if instinctive from birth. He pauses for a moment and sits on the edge of his bed as he ponders how his brother fares this day. Only a few years older than himself, his brother, Sam, is somewhere in the Pacific facing the terrors of the Japanese Empire as many a young American man have been for several years now. The little he does know comes from the papers, the news reels at the theater, and the occasional letters he receives from his brother. These thoughts have weighed heavily upon him for some time as he has gone about his days, but they have grown in both their weight and regularity, having recently received news that his oldest brother,

THE COAL MAN'S ELDEST BROTHER, Frank, shortly before leaving for the war in Europe.

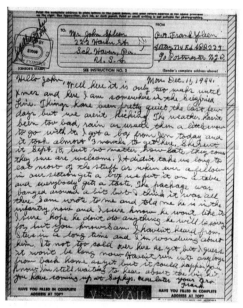

A COPY OF ONE OF THE LAST LETTERS RE-
CEIVED BY THE COAL MAN FROM HIS BROTHER
DURING WWII.

Frank, recently died in Europe at the hands of the Nazi war machine. As he understands it, Frank, who survived the D-day invasion at Normandy, was killed by the machine gun fire of a Nazi warplane while crossing a field to fill his canteen with water from a nearby stream. He came to this fate in the early days of, what is becoming known as the "Battle of the Bulge." But then, who really knows, other than God himself. All he knows for sure is that he will never see his oldest brother again, the brother who was a father figure to him and his other siblings ever since their father passed away when he was just a small boy, no more than six years of age.

He recalls the day when he last saw Sam, saying his farewell at the train station before he boarded a train to leave for training camp. He still struggles with the conflict of his feelings toward his brother that day. A mixture of both love and distain. The love is easily understood, but the sense of distain is still difficult for him to reconcile. It was just the previous evening when Sam showed up at his door in a miserable drunken state, having just wrecked his car. But at least he was still alive; unfortunately, Sam was now there to borrow his car. Despite his misgivings considering the clear fact that Sam was in no condition to be driving, Sam made a good case, passionately pleading that in the coming months he would more than likely die in the war anyway, and they would never see each other again. Although Sam had wanted his brother to join him for a few drinks at the Cotton Club (a local social and drinking establishment), he declined, but in the end yielded to his brother's original request, surrendering the keys to his car. As fate would have it, Sam went on to also wreck the Coal Man's car later that night. He would live through that wreck also, and ultimately go on to survive the Japanese.

His wife Emma remains pleasantly sleeping while he dresses and heads downstairs for some coffee and to freshen up for the start of his day with a quick shave and wash of his face and hands. For breakfast he supplements his coffee with a donut prior to starting the day. It's a brisk winter morning as he heads out into the elements, seeing little more than his breath illuminated by only the moonlight as he walks into the darkness toward his coal truck. The truck is already loaded from the prior evening with six ton of coal and is ready to head off for the Bronx in New York City. He climbs into the cab of his truck, and after only a few attempts with the ignition, the engine to his red coal truck starts. While he waits for the engine to warm up this cold winter morning, he reminds himself of his good fortune, for the place he is in, and all he has: a loving wife, children, and steady work. While both his brothers went off to war, the nature of his business is considered critical to the war effort by the government. As such, it has resulted in several deferments from serving in this tragic world conflict that has imposed itself upon everyone he knows.

Although the war has resulted in many hardships, including the deaths of loved ones for many Americans, he understands that conditions are far worse for those in the war zones, combatants and civilians alike. But can he fully comprehend it? Can anyone other than those who are living through the hell of it all? What he does know from his own personal life experiences is that just a few years earlier, prior to the war, he grew up through the depths of the Great Depression. Raised principally by only his mother and eldest brother, he entered grade school speaking only Italian. English came to him quickly, however, and although he fared well as a student who was eager to learn, the realities of life would intercede and cause him to leave school in the sixth grade to help support the family. From as far back as he can remember, one of his many chores was to walk along the railroad tracks with a bucket and collect pieces of coal that fell from the rail cars that transported coal from the Pennsylvania mining town of Pottsville to Reading, Philadelphia, and other points beyond. The coal he collected was the sole source of heat from a cast iron coal stove in the small apartment where he lived with his mother, three brothers, and sister. This same coal stove is where his mother prepared their meals each day. But that was then, and in a short time, after a few years working for another coal delivery man, he now owns his own coal truck, and in the entrepreneurial spirit of the American dream, he now owns and runs his own coal delivery business.

This day will be a typical run for him, approximately 150 miles each way (taking about eight hours round trip), which he typically does five to six days a week, sometimes seven during winters such as this. This coal truck is his pride and joy, only after Emma and the kids. The open top body, which holds the six ton of coal, was constructed of rough-cut timbers that were assembled by his own hands, which also painted it red. It's a standard shift without power steering, but it has a good radio that keeps him company on these trips. Eisenhower is currently the Supreme Commander of the Allied forces in the European Theater, and it will be another ten to fifteen years until construction of the Interstate Highway system is under way. Until that time arrives, he will be driving two lane roads (one each way), taking Route 61 from Schuylkill Haven, in the heart of Pennsylvania's coal region, to route 22, through Allentown, Pennsylvania, across the Delaware River, the breadth of New Jersey, to the George Washington Bridge, and across the Hudson River into New York City.

A few hours later, it's dawn as he arrives in the Bronx, New York. The sun had started to rise about a half-hour earlier as he approached the city from New Jersey. He has three stops this morning. The first is a three ton delivery of nut coal; the second is one ton of stove coal, and the last, another two-ton of nut. (The terms nut and stove refer to the gradation size of the pieces of coal, each piece of nut coal is the approximate size of a chestnut, hence the name. Stove coal is larger, with each piece of stove coal the approximate size of a small egg.) Each of these deliveries are separated in the back of his truck by movable bin dividing planks, which he set up and loaded the previous evening. The bed of his truck can be reconfigured for any delivery of multiple/combination of one-ton units, up to six ton.

His first stop is at a small deli, where he is greeted by the owner with a cup of coffee, which is of considerable comfort since the air is quite brisk after stepping from the heated cab of his truck. He wastes little time with formalities, thanking the gentleman for his generosity and proceeding to remove his coal chutes from the rear of the truck's under-carriage. This will be his most straightforward delivery of the day, since gravity will do most of the work for him. With the bottom of his truck bed being almost four feet above the ground and the close proximity of the truck to the basement window that leads to his customer's coal bin, the slope of his chutes, when properly set-up, will allow the coal to flow freely down the chute to its destination in the building's basement.

Slide-door pockets built into the bottom sides of his truck bed will also assist by allowing the coal to fall freely from his truck to the chutes.

Within short order his chutes are set in place, supported by wooden milk crates; whereupon, he opens the slide-door in the truck bed releasing the coal to begin flowing from the truck, down the chute, and into the basement. This will continue unimpeded for almost fifteen minutes, or through about half of the three tons of coal, at which point, as the coal bin begins to fill, the pile of coal in the basement causes the coal flowing down the chute to back up and bring the operation to a stop. Now, the Coal Man needs to go down into the basement and shovel the buildup of coal away from the chute, allowing it to again continue to flow freely. Not long after the coal begins flowing, it stops again, this time not because of a back-up in the basement, but because all the coal for this delivery that could flow and fall directly from his truck bed through the slide-door to the chute has run out. The Coal Man now needs to go back up to his truck, climb up into the truck's bed, and shovel the remaining coal to the slide-door pocket and down the chute.

This process of climbing down from the truck bed, going down into the basement to shovel coal from the chute, walking back upstairs, and climbing back up onto his truck to shovel coal to the chute will repeat several times until the balance of the three tons reach their destination in the basement coal bin. A little less than halfway through this process, the Coal Man had forgotten about the cold weather and had to remove a layer of his outer garments since his work began to provide more warmth than was needed by his heavy clothing. Before getting back into his truck to head off for his next delivery, the deli owner provides the Coal Man with a slice of apple pie, along with his payment for the coal, and thanks him for the coal that will keep him and his customers warm through the balance of this winter.

His second delivery, which is only a short drive away, is to the home of a woman whose husband, like his brothers, is off fighting in the war. It is now nearly 8:00 a.m. as he arrives and sees her getting her two children off for school. This delivery, although only one ton, will be one of his more difficult because the home sits on the slope of a hill on the high side of the street relative to where he will park his truck. Therefore, to get adequate slope on his chutes for the coal to flow freely, he will be unable to make use of the slide-door pockets in the bed of his truck. Instead, he will need to rest the high end of the chutes on top of the truck bed sidewalls and shovel the full ton of coal from the truck into the chute. Making matters more difficult is the fact that this is "stove coal" (the largest gradation of coal), which is the most difficult to shovel by hand. All things considered as he starts off with his shoveling, it's not terribly difficult because the coal is at the top of the truck bed's side walls, so all he needs to do is throw the coal horizontally into the chute, but as he progresses, with each shovel full, he will need to heave the coal higher to get it over the truck bed sidewalls. By the time he reaches the bottom of the truck bed he will be heaving each shovel full of coal above his head to get it into the chute. But then this is the nature of the business he has chosen for himself, and instead of giving such details much thought, he proceeds without hesitation, taking pride in his work and the accomplishment he feels at the completion of each delivery.

He has been making this delivery for several years now, and as usual she greets him with more coffee and some cookies she had made the night before. Providing refreshments such as this is a common practice for most of his customers, and the main reason for his eating such a light

breakfast before leaving home. He easily burns through the many cal-
ories over the course of his typical mornings. This woman is generally
very conversational, and true to form, she starts by telling him of the
latest letter she received from her husband. As she speaks, he wastes
no time eating the cookies and washing them down with the coffee. He
then politely thanks her for her hospitality and excuses himself to get to
work. Normally, he would engage her in some small talk, but today he
fears that the conversation may migrate to his brother Frank's death in
Europe, cause for him to keep the conversation short. Not so much for
himself, but for her sake, he wants to avoid sharing this most recent and
unfortunate news, particularly since somewhere in Europe is where her
husband now is.

Although this delivery requires continued difficult shoveling, it is only
one ton, and affords him the additional benefit of not needing to climb
back and forth, off and on the truck, to clear coal from the chute in the
basement like he needed to do on the prior delivery. Additionally, he
has been fortunate this winter's day since there was no precipitation the
night before, which causes the coal to freeze together. When this happens, before he can begin off-loading any delivery, he needs to get out
his pickax to break apart and break free the coal that would be frozen together and frozen to the side walls of the truck bed. Ironically, he prefers
orders larger than a single ton; two, four, or even six tons is preferable,
the larger the better because it means less stops. However, this woman,
as with many of his residential customers, is still recovering from the
Great Depression. To make ends meet they spread the cost for their fuel
over multiple one-ton deliveries each season.

Before he collects his payment and leaves this stop, there is one other order of business. During the Christmas season each year, he supplements

his income by hauling Christmas trees, along with the coal, from the mountains in Pennsylvania to his customers in the city, and this woman is one of his costumers who had ordered a tree during his last delivery to her. So, he climbs back up onto the truck to retrieve the tree and carries it into the house. The satisfaction of the additional income this brings to the Coal Man's family for the Christmas holiday is doubled by the smiles on the faces of his customers, such as this woman as he places the tree in the corner of her living room.

To further supplement his income, in the dead of winter, on weekends or days when travel to make his deliveries may have been too hazardous due to inclement weather, he would go to "Willow Lake" to cut and pack ice. Willow Lake was a moderately sized resort area conveniently located within walking distance from where he and Emma lived. In the summers, the lake was alive with families swimming and picnicking. There was a playground and amusements for the children, and in the evenings, there was a large dance hall overlooking the lake, where people came and danced to the music of the big bands. Harvesting ice from the lake dovetailed well into his own business. The ice was harvested primarily on the most bitter of cold winter days, which coincided with the days where the weather was not as cooperative with the operation of his coal truck. The nature of the work being very much weather-dependent also meant that the need for the labor force required to cut and pack the ice was not steady, and the Coal Man and others were hired on as day laborers. Although by the 1940s much work was beginning to be mechanized, the ice from the lake was still cut by hand saws, drawn from the lake on sleds pulled by draft animals, and manually stacked and packed in straw in a large, warehouse-like sub-basement under the dance hall. It would remain stored there until summer when it would be distributed and sold to families to preserve their food in the kitchen ice boxes of his time.

His final stop is to a business in an industrial area of the Bronx. At this delivery, the basement window to the coal bin is at the back of the building where there is no direct access for his truck. In fact, where he must park his truck is nearly a hundred yards from where the coal needs to go, making his chutes of little use. In this situation he will need to set up one short chute through the basement window to the coal bin and wheelbarrow the coal from the truck to the back of the building to dump each individual wheelbarrow load into the chute feeding the basement. To off-load the two ton of coal for this delivery, he will make approximately twenty trips back and forth from the truck pushing the wheelbarrow full of coal (weighing approximately 200 lbs. each) a hundred yards to the back of the building to dump it into the chute to the basement, then a hundred yards back to the truck with the empty wheelbarrow to refill it. Fortunately, the grade is level; there are few things more difficult than pushing a wheelbarrow full of coal up hill, although he has done it far more times than he would like to recount.

This may not be his largest delivery of the day, but it will surely take the longest. Besides the time it takes to make each cycle of a wheelbarrow load from the truck to dump it into the chute and back again, he needs to take several breaks to get his wind. Additionally, similar to his first stop of the day, when he is approximately halfway complete with this delivery, he needs to climb up on the truck between wheelbarrow loads to shovel the coal to the slide-door pocked to fill each wheelbarrow load. While not tall in stature, this young man, the son of Italian immigrants, is a strapping physical specimen from his early years of hard labor such as this. He has grown accustomed to the work such that he has adapted to the daily aches, pains, and muscle fatigue that he gives little thought to anymore. Anyway, it's nothing that cannot be addressed with a few aspirin at the end of the day. While the work is indeed hard, at least he never had to work in the mines as many of his friends and his wife's brothers have. Some have lost their lives to mining accidents, and others will succumb to ailments, such as black lung disease, in their later years as a result of their years of inhaling coal dust.

It takes a little less than an hour until he empties his last wheelbarrow full of coal into the chute that feeds the coal into the basement coal bin. He returns to the truck to stow the chute he used for this delivery, securing it to the underside of the truck bed and loading his wheelbarrow up into the back of the truck, and after receiving payment and scheduling his next delivery with this customer, he is back on the road and heading home. It is a little after 10:00 a.m. when he finally pulls out, knowing that it will be another three hours before he reaches home, hoping to have time for lunch with his wife when he arrives. About two hours later after crossing the Delaware river, he has less than an hour's worth of driving left. Today's drive has gone well, having no mechanical issues with the truck or flat tires. Getting a flat tire has become all too common, and it is now nearly an expected occurrence that happens on almost half of his trips. The cause of this is also attributable to the war, which seems to have crept into almost every aspect of life. More specifically, the war has caused a rationing of things deemed critical to the war effort, such as fuel and rubber. Ever since the start of the war, both fuel and tires have been rationed.

Due to the nature of his business being critical to the war effort by keeping the supply of coal from the mines to cities such as New York, the government provides him with a reasonably ample supply of rationing coupons for the fuel necessary to make his deliveries, but new tires are another story. They have been very hard to come by due to the rationing of rubber products, which are essential and in high demand for much of the necessary equipment and tools of war being manufactured to supply the troops in Europe and the South Pacific. The supply of natural rubber has been severely limited since more than 90% of it came from Southeast Asia, which is now under the control of the Empire of Japan. Although somewhat exaggerated, he jokes that his truck tires are held together more by the many patches he has applied than the original rubber used to make them.

When he arrives home, as expected his wife awaits him with lunch. It is a simple lunch, consisting of a ham-and-cheese sandwich and a warm bowl of soup, but its simplicity is easily lost by this hungry man's appetite on a cold winter's day. Indeed, it is delicious, welcome, and difficult to comprehend anything that could be equally as satisfying. As much as he may be enjoying his lunch, he can't help but smell the sauce Emma has slow cooking on the back of the stove. She is preparing a tomato marinara sauce with the rabbit that he brought home the prior weekend after a day of hunting with his dog, Pal. Yes, this evening he will be dining on spaghetti with tomato/rabbit sauce. He is fond of spaghetti, and although of Italian descent, he has an equally opposite dislike for pizza. As he describes it, as a child it seemed that pizza was all he ever had to eat, and this gave him the view that pizza was the Italian version of poor people's food. Making matters worse, it seemed that his mother almost always made it with those "little fishes" (anchovies) on it, which he disliked with a passion! It's not long before he has completed this meal, but before getting back on the road, he takes a few minutes and goes to the kennel in the backyard to feed Pal, who will feast on the table scraps

Emma collected from the prior day. As Pal laps up his lunch, the Coal Man wonders if Pal will enjoy the scraps from this evening's coming pasta dinner with the rabbit sauce as much as he will. When he and Pal go hunting, it's rarely a question of whether they will bring home some game, but more a question of how many pheasants and/or rabbits they will bring home.

Then, it's back in his truck, and he is on his way up to the mines. This is a short drive, taking less than a half hour, and upon his arrival, he pulls his truck onto a large scale where the weight of the empty truck is recorded. After his truck is weighed there is a short wait since there are a few other independent delivery trucks waiting in line to be loaded. When it comes to his turn, he pulls his truck alongside a large structure built into the hillside, which houses the raw coal that has been brought up from the mines by rail carts. The structure is at a higher elevation, which allows the coal to flow freely into the bed of his truck when a chute is lowered. Although this process is nearly automatic, making use of gravity to load his truck, he still needs to climb up into the truck to help spread the full six tons of coal out evenly with his shovel in the truck's bed. The noise of this large volume of coal rapidly passing through the metal chute to his truck is intensely loud, but these are the days before ear protection, and it will take a toll on his hearing in the years to come. When full, he pulls his truck back onto the scale to again be weighed. In this way, they can confirm the weight of the coal loaded by subtracting the empty truck's weight (obtained when he arrived), from the loaded weight of the truck. It is this weight that his payment for the coal is based upon.

His truck now filled with six tons of raw coal from the mines, he heads home, knowing that the real work of his day is about to begin. But first, he must make a stop to pick up some items for dinner with Emma this

Friday evening. In addition to the few items from a list she gave him at lunch, he also gets two bottles of Coca-Cola and a bag of loose pretzels (he buys the broken pretzels, which are sold at a discount to the whole pretzels), to be enjoyed while he and his wife are entertained by listening to their stories or big band music on the radio as is their custom on Friday evenings. On occasion they will hear updates on the war from President Roosevelt, who gives what will come to be known as his fireside chats with the Nation.

When he arrives home, he stops at the house to give his wife the groceries he picked up earlier and catches a whiff of the sauce still slow cooking on the back of the stove, but there's no time to take a break. It's already 3:00 p.m., and he has much hard work ahead of him before he can sit down for dinner with Emma and the kids. He therefore heads back out, the temperature not as brisk as when he first left earlier that morning. Across the street is a small abandoned quarry where he had parked the truck upon his return from the mines. On the side of the hill adjacent to his truck, but at an elevation slightly higher than the truck, are a series of coal bins, which he uses to sort the various sizes of coal that he delivers each day to his customers based on their individual needs (i.e. the type of coal necessary for the type of stove or heater they may have). The coal in his truck is known as "raw coal," meaning that it is still in the form that it was when originally extracted from the mine, consisting of a mixture of sizes from small pieces to large chunks. He must shovel this coal from the truck to one of the bins on the hillside where he will break it up with a sledge hammer, then, with sieves having various gradations of screening, he will sieve it into other bins — each holding a specific size or gradation of coal. It takes him little more than an hour to shovel the raw coal off the truck and begin the work of breaking and sieving it, keeping a careful eye out for foreign objects that on occasion may be mixed in with the coal. There are even occasions where he had found undetonated blasting caps. This possibility adds a heightened sense of diligence and caution to this task. He hardly notices the drop in temperature as evening begins to set in, his work providing more than ample warmth. His concern now becomes more focused on the amount of daylight that remains. As the sun inevitably starts to set, he is just beginning to reload the truck by shoveling the graded, or sized, coal back into the truck for tomorrow's delivery. When darkness does set in, he lights a coal oil lamp, which will provide the lighting needed to finish his work for the day.

It is now nearly 6:00 p.m. when he finishes reloading the truck and returns to the house. He washes up for dinner, and after a very satisfying meal of spaghetti and rabbit marinara sauce with Emma and the kids, he retires to the living room while his wife cleans up after dinner and puts the children to bed. She joins him shortly thereafter to listen to the radio and enjoy the Coca-Cola and broken pretzels he purchased earlier that day for this occasion. Tomorrow is Saturday, and he has a local delivery scheduled, which is his norm on weekends as it allows him extra time for some hunting in the afternoon. In the spring and summer months, his Saturday afternoons are usually spent fishing or on the many household maintenance chores that occupy the balance of his weekends. His one vice, other than his Lucky Strike cigarettes, is gambling. In fact, much of the correspondence with his brothers during the war is about their success in cards and/or craps (dice). So tomorrow evening he may also head up to Pottsville to try his luck in a game of cards with his friends; Emma refers to this activity as "Crudding" but knows that he's earned this little bit of leisure entertainment at the end of the week since his work resumes when Monday morning arrives. Within less than an hour he is falling asleep on the sofa with Emma, so the two of them retire to bed. It has been another long but typical day in the life of the Coal Man, and this man needs his sleep!

THE COAL MAN'S BAPTISMAL CERTIFICATE –
Written in Italian you may note the name
"Giovanni Cupidina." How it became John Spleen
remains somewhat a mystery, although it sounds
much more American, and maybe that was the
intent.

Postscript: The preceding story is a true story, if not in the literal sense of a particular day in the life of the Coal Man. It is true insofar as it is a compilation of stories passed to this author by his grandfather. I was fortunate enough to have been born the eldest grandchild to the man identified above as the "Coal Man." His name was John Spleen Sr., and as a child, I would ride with him on his red coal truck. In later years, during college and even beyond, I would help him on many of his deliveries for extra money. He was always very generous in most things, but exceedingly so when it came to my pay. Although the work was indeed awfully hard, I was without question very overpaid for the assistance I brought to bear. It was during this much valued one-on-one quality time that I had the opportunity to spend with him on his coal truck and hunting or fishing that I was able to compile and commit to memory the antidotes he shared with me. The stories he told of his youth and early life were provided in an unembellished matter-of-fact manner. "That's just how it was," and that's just how I have attempted to portray a man whom I respected and loved beyond what I can describe in words. It has also presented me with the opportunity to illustrate the work ethic that was as much a part of his identity as it was for many other Americans of his time.

Therefore, I believe the foregoing story, or more accurately compilation of stories, provide an accurate representation of a given day in his life in the early 1940s. Furthermore, it was the work ethic and virtues he projected that later in my life would drive my own work ethic. On late evenings early in my career, far too many to count, when others had already left work hours earlier for the day, I would start to question my own stamina and whether my work ethic was misguided. It was at times such as this that I would remind myself that even my longest, most challenging, and most difficult of days were in no way comparable, by any measure, to what my grandfather endured on an average workday.

One more note on this man; I really don't know what he listened to on that AM radio on those long days in his coal truck back in the 1940s, but rather than guess, what I can say is that when I would ride with him as a child in the 60s and later as a young man in the late 70s and early 80s, much to my delight, he would put on rock 'n' roll music. Not sure if he did this just for me or if he liked it also, but I do recall him mentioning that he did like The Beatles, particularly their song "I Want to Hold Your Hand." I also recall fond memories of the two of us singing that song together in the cab of that red Coal Truck.

Finally, if you have not already guessed it, the man pictured on the cover of this book is John Spleen Sr., the "Coal Man," once upon a time in the "Good Old Days," fishing a stream somewhere in the Pennsylvania mountains of Schuylkill County.

Epilogue

"What doesn't kill you only makes you stronger."
—*Friedrich Nietzsche*

Our society has evolved so rapidly and so dramatically in just two hundred years that it is difficult for us today to comprehend the hardships endured by generations just fifty to one hundred years ago, let alone one hundred fifty to two hundred years past. Recent generations have grown accustomed to receiving trophies just for showing up, and the appeasement of an ever-growing population of easily offended and hurt feelings has led to college campuses with "Safe Spaces" and socially imposed limitations on speech. More and more we are living in an illusion, devoid of the realities of the human condition. Although much of the reality of the true hardship that humanity has endured through ages past has, for the most part, been preserved in the historical record, it rarely sees the light of day. Yet today in portions of the world it is still all too vivid and omnipresent, places where reality will hit you squarely in the face. In Venezuela, you know you're in a slump when food shortages are so profound that all the zoo animals have been eaten and there's no toilet paper to wipe your ass! And in many places around the world conditions are even far worse.

Through this work I have attempted to present, in the foregoing chapters, information and thoughts about subject matter that here-to-for has lingered in the shadows of history, not readily entering the consciousness of many, and I'll even go as far as to say most. The nature of some of the foregoing content may have been found by some to be distasteful or even repulsive, and in fact to some degree, that may well have been in part my intent. No efforts were made toward "political correctness," but at the same time, I had no deliberate intent to offend. My intent was to write plainly in an effort to achieve clarity on subject matter that has readily and easily been obscured by the façade of our modern-day society. While fashionable in recent years, the currently overused phrase "just trying to start a conversation" is appropriately accurate in this context. I have endeavored to provide better context for our place in time, as food for thought, and to instill a desire to obtain a better understanding of historical context. In turn, it is my hope to cultivate greater substantive political engagement in our society by those who have read my work.

In 1774, on the eve of the American War for Independence against Great Britain, one of John Adams journal entries reads:

> "I wander alone and ponder. I muse, I mope, I ruminate. We have
> not men fit for the times. We are deficient in genius, education,
> in travel, fortune — in everything. I feel unutterable anxiety."

When John Adams wrote these words, he and others of the founding generation were surely faced with a future of uncertainty that few today can begin to fathom. The potential for war against the greatest and most formidable military and naval power the world had known to his time. To him and his peers, the perils it presented were vivid and well within sight. If they failed, their fate was worse than mere death; the penalty under the crown for treason in his day was to be hanged, drawn and quartered, with your body parts being displayed on pikes in different parts of the land as a deterrence to others. Such was the fate of William Wallace and others, who over the course of English history dared to take up arms against the king. If they succeeded, their fate was far less certain.

If you feel detached from historical events such as this because they seem so distant from your own life, you may be able to gain a greater and more relative perspective of the pace of change for humanity over time by looking at it, not from the statistical aspect of 20-year generational intervals, but from the span of those whose lives overlap with ours. For example, I was born before the last of the Civil War veterans had died, and many of those veterans' lives overlapped with those of the founding of the United States. From this perspective, we see ourselves little more than two lifetimes from those of the Founding Fathers. Another perspective on just how rapid the advancement of society has been over the past 250 years is a simple comparison to the 250 years prior. If we use 1492 as a benchmark, a year we all know of as marking Christopher Columbus's discovery of America, it becomes obvious that the advancement in the condition of mankind was nearly negligible for the nearly 300 years from the time of Columbus up to the founding of the American Republic, its democracy, and the engine of its free enterprise system, or capitalism, for the nearly 250 years that followed.

It is hardly conceivable that the rapid advancement of the past 250 years could have been achieved under the monarchies of early 1800s Europe or later Marxist doctrine. All that we hold dear, and far greater, and all that we take for granted is the product George Washington's six-year life and death struggle with the English Crown. The efforts of the many other Founders, putting onto paper, and into practice, the most innovative republican form of democracy the world has come to know, and the dogged persistence of Alexander Hamilton in building the foundation for the free enterprise, capitalistic system that delivered it all. Had they not achieved what they had, it is not beyond reason that many of us would still be shitting in the woods and wiping our butts with our hands and the water from a stream that was hopefully nearby. Progressivism has steadily and increasingly been growing government and eroding freedoms, thereby handcuffing initiative and stifling innovation. The Founders put into place a form of central government intended to be, and originally established, as small and unobtrusive as possible, allowing free enterprise to flourish. We have steadily been approaching a tipping point, and I'm not referring to global warming or climate change. It's the potential of undoing the considerable advancements achieved over the past 200 years.

In an effort to summarize the thrust of the preceding chapters, consider the following either literally or in any relative form that you may better relate to. When was the last time you were awakened in the middle of the night by the sound of a bell being rung by a man in the street? A man pulling a cart full of corpses and crying out; "BRING OUT YOUR DEAD!?" Or when was the last time you had difficulty sleeping due to fears of roving marauders who might burn your home, take all your worldly possessions, rape and/or abduct your wife and daughters, and hack the life from you and your sons with their swords or battle axes? Or maybe your persistent insomnia is the result of air raid sirens, and the need to find shelter in the subway from the aerial bombing each night. If you are old enough you may recall the double-digit inflation of the late 1970s and early 1980s, but can you begin to comprehend inflation over

100%, 1,000% or 1,000,000%? The price of goods or services doubling every few days with no opportunity to secure the means necessary to purchase daily necessities regardless of price. Or for that matter, no conceivable prospect to better your or your children's stations in life. Let's be clear, we're not just speaking of some relative measure of difficulty, but an absolute impossibility! When was the last time you contemplated the need of wearing a gas mask to protect yourself from the dense and deadly smog outside, or had given any thought whatsoever about the potential health effects of the water you drink? When was the last time you had concerns or given thought to the possibility of being eaten by a wild animal or, worse, being eaten by your friends or neighbors who are near death from starvation? As disconcerting as current news of the political antics being played out may at times seem, when was the last time you heard of a politician challenging another to more than a gentleman's wager or, worse, a debate? Believing I already know the answer to most of these questions, no, all of the foregoing rhetorical rant, it isn't much of a stretch to assume that you have not spent any recent evenings praying late into the night for relief or salvation from anything nearly approaching any of these possibilities. I'll even go further out on a limb and assume that if you're reading this text, your literacy is not in question either. Although the occasional inconsiderate driving of others and traffic may cause you anguish, and at times even considerable anguish, when was the last time you had to change a flat tire? Do you even know how? If you ever had to suffer through broken air conditioning on a hot day, how inhumane a torture was that? And if you haven't heard from your teenager at college in weeks, it's probably not due to delays in the delivery of your mail. Has hunger ever driven you to the point of remotely considering that scraps of food in a city trash can or dumpster could satisfy your appetite? And when was the last time you spent any length of time sleeping in the woods? If you have, how heavenly and luxurious was that first shower that you took after returning home?

Comparatively, the considerable majority of issues and/or challenges confronting us today, both public and private, are minor in nature when set side by side with those faced by our predecessors. Unfortunately, nearly any measure of hardship, no matter how slight, is often sensationalized and over-dramatized by extremes of hyperbole for effect. Note the rise in recent years of the incorrect use of the word "literally" as an adjective. As if the English language is short on adjectives. On the other hand, issues and/or challenges of consequence are often shrouded in disinformation, and if not merely glossed over, they are generally avoided or downplayed if they do not support a favored narrative. As a society and starting as individuals it has become increasingly important that we exercise a healthy degree of skepticism and a rational perspective, particularly with the growth of technology and social media driving the information overload most of us experience daily.

Shortly after the founding of the United States, democracy and free market capitalism began to spread throughout most of Europe and other parts of the world. Its spread continued through the end of World War II, with the defeat of European fascism and Imperial Japan, and later into parts of Eastern Europe with the fall of the Soviet Union. It is difficult for most of us today to truly understand the definition of tyranny as it was known to the founders or what it was like to live under despotic rule. Yet today, we get glimpses of it through the lenses of media outlets from countries such as China, Cuba, Venezuela, and Russia.

The fact is that historically, and in general, conditions are very good if not exceptionally good for most of the populations of North America,

Europe, and Australia. The 20th century has seen a paradigm shift in nearly every aspect of what it means to be human. Before the 20th century, mankind surely had the ability to dream, but for the masses, those dreams were limited to what they could comprehend from the world they lived in. Therefore, it is unlikely that any dreams they did have could go much beyond their basic needs for survival. In contrast, our dreams today are limited only by the boundaries of our imagination. The American Dream is whatever you perceive it to be, and not some abstraction proclaimed for you by others. It is more about the opportunity available to attain those dreams, whatever they may be, from the abundance of our present-day society. It is in this new paradigm that the only thing standing between anyone and their dreams is a pervasive pretension of victimhood. Escaping this "victim mentality" requires that we not only break out of our own self-imposed bubbles, but also break through those created by a political class and the mass media. The poll tested, manipulative rhetoric spewed by all too many a politician, filtered, propagated, and enhanced with hyperbole for marketing effect by the media, is all the more further filtered, propagated, and enhanced by the technology we hold in our hands every day. An unfortunate reality is that if we have enough people repeatedly telling us how bad things are and that we are all victims, we will invariably start believing it. In the words of Lincoln, the American form of government is intended to be *"of the people, by the people, and for the people"*; however, politics is rarely about the people, contrary to the pleadings of many a politician; it is in reality about power. Contrary to prevailing assertions, there is no other place or time in which minorities of any persuasion have realized such equality of opportunity. The same is true for women who through time, and still today in too many parts of the world, have been viewed as the property of their fathers, then their husbands, beyond which prostitution was one of the few alternative opportunities.

We can and should count our blessings for all those who have come before us and their collective efforts that have provided us with the most prosperous times known to mankind. And while it is altogether appropriate to renew our appreciation for this fact, at the same time, we need to remain cognizant that their efforts were not necessarily directed toward the wellbeing of future generations (i.e. us) but guided by their own self-interests. Similarly, it is us acting in our own self-interests that we will provide a brighter future for those who follow. The natural human inclination for self-preservation and to act in one's own self-interests is unfortunately, generally, viewed solely in a negative light. As powerful a force as self-interest can be evil, its power is no less a considerable force for good; however, it is rarely recognized as such. Isn't it much more logical that our efforts and energies will have far less impact when focused on the appeasement of the perceived needs of others, as opposed to directing greater focus on our own wellbeing? How can we expect to assist our children or others if we are not first secure in our own right? The airlines remind us of this fundamental fact at the start of every flight when the flight attendant provides the routine flight safety instructions, which include a portion that goes somewhat like this:

> *"In the unlikely event of a loss in cabin pressure, your oxygen masks will drop from the overhead compartment. First place your mask on your face, tightly pulling the straps on each side to secure it before assisting your children or others."*

In plain English, how should anyone expect to genuinely have any expectation of helping anyone else if they don't first have their own shit together? Once we've recognized and succeeded in this fundamental, the ability for further advancement is largely dependent upon an accurate understanding of present conditions relative to those that preceded them.

It is my hope that in some measure this book will provide the impetus to break through your bubble and engage beyond the day-to-day. Make the effort to understand history, the lives, sacrifices, and the achievements of those that came before you. Be cognizant of current events, both those near and far, because even the most remote may have the potential to influence your life. And when it comes to politics, only a fool is either ambivalent or a zealot. The zealots who typically work at the extreme fringe of society generally have little effect since they are rarely taken seriously, but if they find an opportunity and/or are enabled to exert authority, the ambivalent become their victims. Zealotry does not necessarily imply evil intent; in fact, I would venture to guess that most zealots are generally well-intentioned ideologues, albeit misguided. The unintended consequences of their unchecked actions can, and often are, counter to their original intended goals. To this regard, two famous quotes come to mind: the first by Edmond Burke, who said, *"The only thing necessary for the triumph of evil is for good men to do nothing,"* and the second for which the origin is disputed, *"The road to hell is paved with good intentions."*

So, the next time you hear someone make the statement that the current, or next generation, will be the first generation that will not be better off than its predecessor, you will know that they are either being willfully disingenuous or suffer a foolish ignorance. But there is no need to be so forthright, simply ask in turn, "What about the generation of all those who came of age during the prosperity of the 'Roaring Twenties' only to see the collapse of the stock market in 1929? Then going on to live through or, better put, to survive the 'Great Depression' over the subsequent decade, which was followed by the Second World War in the 1940s. Has the generation previously known as 'Greatest Generation' already been forgotten?"

One Final Perspective

Around 2,000 years ago, the greatest civilization to that time in human history flourished. Today we easily look back upon it and readily see the many flaws of that society, often overlooking the achievements attained by that same society. A society built upon military conquest, with much of its population enslaved. The oppression and persecution of a new religion, Christianity, and the crucifixion of Jesus Christ. And entertainment for the masses consisting of macabre spectacles and contests of brutality and death. On the other hand, this civilization mastered great feats of engineering: aqueducts that brought fresh water to the cities from distant mountain sources, roads connecting the far reaches of the empire, and architecture that inspires awe yet today. There were great advancements and achievements in nautical engineering and maritime trade. Advancement of the arts and scholarly pursuits. The ability to construct and support great and populous cities. And a rudimentary republican form of government, all-be-it authoritarian and controlled by many a tyrannical emperor. So, what is the proper perspective; was Rome a great achievement or a regression in the evolution of humanity? Or more simplistically, was it good or evil?

The simplest, and surely an accurate, answer is that it was both at the same time. But surely one's leanings to either end of the spectrum is dependent upon the degree to which our perspective is principally either naive or pragmatically selective, objective, or moralistic. Does this judgement change when we look at what followed the Roman Empire? In other words, was it a good thing for humanity that the Empire fell, or was it unfortunate? This question has been considered by many scholars in the years that followed Rome's fall, and many judgements have been made, but what lessons can we learn? What were the underlying causes of Rome's decline and fall? Irrespective of the many scholarly efforts in attempting to answer these questions, one thing is, however, certain. Rome fell when the barbarians crossed the Rubicon, entered the capital, and sacked the city.

If we allow ourselves to be objective and free of moral judgement on the virtues of the American experiment, could it be that the Rio Grande is North America's modern equivalent of Rome's Rubicon? If so, what could we reasonably expect to follow?

References

◆ Books

Alexis de Tocqueville; Translated by Harvey C. Mansfield & Delba Winthrop. *Democracy in America* (April 1, 2002)

Burstein, Andrew & Isenberg, Nancy. *Madison & Jefferson* (September 28, 2010)

Chernow, Ron. *Alexander Hamilton* (March 29, 2005)

———. *Washington: A Life* (September 27, 2011)

Drury, Bob & Clavin, Tom. *Valley Forge* (October 2, 2018)

Ellis, Joseph. *His Excellency: George Washington* (November 8, 2005)

Freeman, Joanne B. *Affairs of Honor: National Politics in the New Republic* (September 1, 2002)

Friedman, Milton. *Capitalism & Freedom: 40th Anniversary Edition* (November 15, 2002)

Greenspan, Allen. *The Age of Turbulence: Adventures in a New World* (January 1, 2007)

Hamilton, Alexander, Madison, James & Jay, John. *The Federalist* (July 1st, 2001)

Levin, Mark R. *Unfreedom of the Press* (May 21, 2019)

McCullough, David. *John Adams* (September 3, 2002)

———. *1776* (June 27, 2006)

Meacham, Jon. *American Lion: Andrew Jackson in the White House* (November 11, 2008)

———. *Thomas Jefferson: The Art of Power* (October 29, 2013)

Philbrick, Nathaniel. *Bunker Hill: A City, a Siege, a Revolution* (April 30, 2013)

———. *In the Hurricane's Eye: The Genius of George Washington and the Victory at Yorktown* (November 23, 2018)

———. *Valiant Ambition: George Washington, Benedict Arnold, and the Fate of the American Revolution* (May 10, 2016)

Smith, Adam; Edited by: Tony Darnell. *The Wealth of Nations* (January 18, 2018)

Merck & Co. *Merck Manual of Medical Information: Home Edition* (September 1, 1997)

♦ Periodicals

Debter, Lauren. *Relentlessly Rich: The 2018 Forbes 400 by the Numbers* (October 5, 2018)

Rosenwald, Michael S. *History's deadliest pandemics from ancient Rome to modern America: The Washington Post* (April 7, 2020)

♦ Documentary Films

Allitt, Patrick N., PhD. *The Conservative Tradition (The Great Courses)* (2009)

Burns, Ken. *The Civil War* (1990)

Ferguson, Niall, DPhil. *Civilization: The West and the Rest* (2012)

———. *The Ascent of Money: A Financial History of the World* (2009)

Diamond, Jared, PhD. *Guns, Germs & Steel* (2005)

Stein, Ben. *Expelled: No Intelligence Allowed* (2008)

♦ Websites

https://thesurvivaljournal.com

https://www.healthline.com

https://www.cdc.gov

https://ibanplastic.com

https://ourworldindata.org

https://www.history.com

Index

Engage as your forefathers had; consider and explore this:

The need for a Convention of the States to impose term limits on the legislators of both houses of Congress. Preferably a two-term limit, the same as that imposed by the 22nd Amendment on the Executive Branch for office holders of the Presidency. After all, what's good for the goose is good for the gander.

About the Author

Originally raised in the suburban Philadelphia, PA area, Rick has lived on both the East Coast (NYC) and West Coast (LA), and in many states in between, as well as in Mexico and the Caribbean. He moved many times over the course of his career managing major commercial construction projects, such as the Trump Castle in Atlantic City, NJ, and the W.T. Young Library at the University of Kentucky in Lexington, KY. While in California he wrote a monthly political news-letter titled "News from the Left Coast" for a period and was the winner of his age group in the 2016 Long Beach Triathlon. Rick is a student of history and is well read, principally in non-fiction and mostly on the topic of the Revolutionary period of the United States. An outdoorsman who enjoys hunting, fishing, sailing, scuba diving, and skiing, he has returned to his roots in the suburbs of Philadelphia and spends part of his time in Tampa, Florida.